THE ILLUSTRATED HISTORY OF
STOCK
CAR
RACING

DON HUNTER AND AL PEARCE

MBI Publishing Company

DEDICATION

To Bill and Jerry Cannon of Clinton, South Carolina.
Your 37 years of friendship, guidance, and support are
appreciated more than you can imagine. I'll be
forever grateful for that curb-side talk with Big
Al that changed my life for the better.
—*Al Pearce*

First published in 1998 by MBI Publishing Company, 729
Prospect Avenue, PO Box 1, Osceola, WI 54020-0001 USA

MBI Publishing Company books are also available at discounts in bulk
quantity for industrial or sales-promotional use. For details write to
Special Sales Manager at Motorbooks International Wholesalers &
Distributors, 729 Prospect Avenue, PO Box 1, Osceola, WI 54020-
0001 USA.

Library of Congress Cataloging-in-Publication Data

Hunter, Don.
      Illustrated history of stock car racing: from the
      sands of Daytona to Madison Avenue/ Don
      Hunter & Al Pearce.
         p. cm.
      Includes index.
      ISBN 0-7603-0416-5 (alk. paper)
        1. Stock car racing--United States--History. 2.
NASCAR (Association) --History. I. Pearce, Al.
II. Title.
GV1029.9.S74H86   1998
796.72'0973--dc21   98-7612

On the front cover: Legends from three eras grace the cover,
with Richard Petty in his trademark No. 43 Plymouth, Tim Flock
piloting a Kiekhaefer-owned Chrysler 300, and Dale Earnhardt
streaking his No. 3 Monte Carlo down the track.
On the frontispiece: Brothers Bob, Tim, and Fonty Flock pose
for a photo in the early 1950s. *Thomas C. Griffin Collection*
On the title page: The start of the 1957 Southern 500 at Darlington.
Speedy Thompson won the race in a Chevrolet.
On the back cover: Top: Buddy Baker blows the engine in his
Cotton Owens Dodge down the front stretch at Talladega.
Bottom: As this shot of the start of the 1994 Mello Yello 500 at
Charlotte illustrates, close competition has been a hallmark of
NASCAR racing since its inception in 1949.

Edited by Lee Klancher
Designed by Katie L. Sonmor

Printed in China through World Print, Ltd.

CONTENTS

ACKNOWLEDGMENTS 7

INTRODUCTION

A Fateful Day at Daytona 9

ONE: THE 1940S

The Smoke Filled Room 17

TWO: THE 1950S

Strictly Stock Makes it Big 35

THREE: THE 1960S

The Most Dangerous Race Fans in America 51

FOUR: THE 1970S

NASCAR Lights Up 77

FIVE: THE 1980S

Corporate America Goes Racin' 105

SIX: THE 1990S

The Golden Age of Stock Car Racing 141

APPENDICES

Year by Year Summary 175

Heroes 182

Champions 191

INDEX 192

A-5
BWP

ACKNOWLEDGMENTS

My thanks to all race drivers, crews, crew chiefs, owners, sponsors, and tracks who helped me through the years to make the photography in this book possible. Photos published in newspapers, magazines, advertising, books, calendars, and posters have made racers heroes in my book.

My appreciation and "thanks" go to the many publishers, editors, and art directors that have contributed to my success for over 40 years. A job well done and handshake goes to Al Pearce who did the writing in ILLUSTRATED HISTORY OF STOCK CAR RACING. He is one of the greatest writers in automotive reacing. I'm grateful to Tom Cotter who helped Lee Klancher, my editor at MBI Publishing, discover my talent in photography. Also, to a good friend and writer, Ben White.

A special thank you goes to my wife, Jean.
—Don Hunter

Many thanks to Tom Cotter, Al Robinson, and Humpy Wheeler, and to dozens upon dozens of NASCAR owners, drivers, crew chiefs and sponsors for their time, patience and undeniable expertise.
—Al Pearce

The 1968 Daytona 500 featured Richard Petty (43) and Cale Yarborough (21) starting on the front row. Yarborough headed a Ford sweep of the top three positions, passing LeeRoy Yarbrough on the second-to-last lap. On lap 17, Mario Andretti crashed (his third of three consecutive NASCAR appearances ending in wrecks) and took out Buddy Baker, who said, "That guy [Andretti] takes out one or two contenders every time he races down here." Smokey Yunick brought a Chevrolet that the tech inspectors disassembled (including removing the fuel tank) and failed to pass, citing nine violations. Yunick reportedly responded, "Make that ten," and drove the car away.

INTRODUCTION

Live CBS coverage of the historic 1979 Daytona race that featured a race-long fender-to-fender battle, an off-track scuffle, and the greatest name in NASCAR taking home the flag brought through-the-roof ratings. The fact that half the country was snowed in didn't hurt, but stock car racing's television coverage increased dramatically nonetheless. Commentators like noted journalist Brock Yates (shown) became integral parts of countless American's new weekend ritual of watching NASCAR racing on the tube.

ABOVE: Donnie Allison started on the outside pole for the 1979 Daytona 500, one position ahead of number three starter Cale Yarborough. Buddy Baker was on the pole, and Richard Petty started back in 13th.

A Fateful Day at Daytona

It was late in the afternoon of February 18, 1979, at the Daytona International Speedway and Donnie Allison knew exactly what was coming in the next few moments. What he couldn't have possibly known or even imagined was the impact those next few moments would have on the growth of NASCAR stock car racing in the United States.

As the tension built and the laps dwindled down in the 21st annual Daytona 500, Allison knew deep in his heart that Cale Yarborough planned to wreck him. He was so certain he knew what lay ahead that with five laps left, he keyed the "TALK" button on his two-way radio and calmly told car-owner Hoss Ellington he expected Yarborough to do the dirty deed as they approached Turn 3 on the 200th and last lap. His only mistake, Allison ruefully conceded years later, was that he gave Yarborough too much credit for being patient.

When CBS decided to give flag-to-flag live coverage to the 1979 Daytona 500, the network was rewarded with an epic last-lap duel. Throughout the race, Donnie Allison (1) and Cale Yarborough (11) battled wheel-to-wheel. Both had a shot at the checkered flag, but neither would take it.

If years of stock car racing experience had taught Donnie Allison anything, it was that Yarborough probably realized he didn't have enough car at his command to make a clean pass, fair and square. And those same years of experience had taught Allison that Yarborough, a burly, no-neck, short-tempered, ex-football player from South Carolina, would no more honorably take second in the sport's most important race than he'd run from a rattlesnake. But as Yarborough was about to discover, Allison wasn't a man to be trifled with, either.

Overshadowed somewhat by Bobby, his more successful, more popular, and better-known older brother, Donnie Allison was a skilled and gifted racer in his own right. By 1979, a dozen years into his career, he'd already won 17 poles and 10 Winston Cup races. Nine of them were on superspeedways, the other on the half-mile bullring at Bristol, Tennessee. But Allison yearned to win just one Daytona 500, the stock car equivalent of the Indianapolis 500 or the 24 Hours of LeMans. Regardless of what else his resume listed, a 500-mile victory at Daytona Beach in February generally defined a NASCAR racer's career for all time.

"If I'd won that race," he said years later, the regret still heavy in his voice, "it would have meant the world to me. You would have seen a different Donnie Allison if what happened that day hadn't happened like it did." His wife, Pat, must have the patience of a saint. "Is he still talking about that?" she said 18 years later. "It'll always be with him, no question about it."

As the laps clicked off every 45 seconds—10 to go, then nine, then eight, then seven—Allison and Yarborough settled on their strategy. At 200 miles an hour, neither would get a second chance to get it right. At the same time they were sizing up each other, the talking heads at CBS television were about to earn their money.

TELEVISION STEPS UP

By February 1979, sportscaster Ken Squier had been around motorsports for almost 25 years. He'd broadcast thousands of races on radio and television, everything from county fair demolition derbies to figure-eight races, from the Indy car circuit to sprint cars and midgets. It seemed altogether appropriate that he would be in the broadcast booth to provide words for what many people now feel was one of the defining moments in American motorsports history.

Squier and sports car racer David Hobbs were in Daytona Beach because CBS had been the first network to agree to a live, start-to-finish telecast of a major stock car race. CBS had picked the Daytona 500 because it was NASCAR's most important event and, truth be told, there weren't many other quality events on Sunday afternoons that time of year. CBS had done some edited-for-time stock car races and a few Indy car shows, but that smattering wasn't nearly enough to satisfy America's growing appetite for motorsports on television.

For CBS, the opportunity to get the Daytona 500 was too good to turn down. "One of the questions around our offices in the mid-1970s was what more could we do in racing," Squier said years later, when asked how it all came about. "When I said we should do Daytona live, Barry Frank became very enthused. The concept of taking the biggest stock car race in the world and treating it like the biggest event of any other sport was a great challenge.

"The producer of that first show was Bob Pearlman and the director was Bob Stenner. They set out to afford Daytona and race fans the same respect and dignity and thoroughness that CBS gave the World Series, the Masters, the Super Bowl, and the Olympics. They were the big events back then, those few and maybe the U.S. Open Tennis, the NBA finals, and any heavyweight fight with Ali. But in 1979, racing wasn't anywhere near that same class."

At the time, NASCAR had a strong and cordial working relationship with ABC. But Frank and fellow CBS executive Neil Pilson flew to Daytona Beach and convinced Bill France Sr. to give them the 500. They closed the deal by assuring France and his staff that CBS would bring the same personnel and technical resources to the Daytona 500 they brought to their other major sports telecasts.

"Two or three things came together to make that race so important," Squier said. "One was the weather in the eastern United States. A huge snowstorm kept tens of thousands of people from driving from the Northeast down to Daytona Beach that weekend. Those people were cabin-bound race fans, so it was natural they'd watch the race. But there wasn't much of anything else on that day, so the 500 almost had a captive audience in the Eastern and Northeastern parts of the country.

"And there was the Foyt issue. Back then, in 1979, A.J. was just about the biggest name in American racing. Everybody knew about him and what he did, based on his success at Indianapolis. The race kept building and building all that afternoon, getting better and better. You had Cale and Donnie running up front, you had Richard Petty and Darrell Waltrip behind them, and then you had A.J. back there, just hanging around, waiting for something to happen. It was a really good race, the kind that kept your attention."

It was, as things turned out, a 500-mile race that kept Americans riveted to their television sets all afternoon, and then even after the checkered flag fell over the unexpected winner.

BATTLE ROYALE

Through hook or crook, or perhaps just bad information, Allison and Ellington went into the final stages of the 500 believing their chief rival was a lap behind. Yarborough had been involved in a couple of minor incidents that had cost him laps, but had been fast enough to make up most of them. So it was that Allison didn't put up much of a fight when Yarborough unlapped himself moments before a late-race caution. Both Ellington and Allison believed Yarborough was still a lap down and no threat. Besides, they felt they'd win the race regardless of where Yarborough was being scored.

"Hell, I didn't think one lap would make any difference," Allison explained. "We'd both wrecked early, but our cars were still in pretty good shape. I could have held Cale back if I'd tried, but we thought he was still a couple of laps behind. That's why I was so aggravated when Hoss came on the radio and said NASCAR had just told him that Cale was back on the lead lap. If I'd known that, he wouldn't have made up that lap. And if he hadn't made up that lap, nothing that happened on the last lap would have happened, and I would have won the Daytona 500."

Allison and Yarborough took the white flag running one and two, Allison's No. 1 Hawaiian Tropic-sponsored Oldsmobile barely ahead of Yarborough's No. 11 Busch-sponsored Oldsmobile. Allison was determined to keep Yarborough stuck in the outside groove through Turns One and Two, making him work hard for whatever he got. He was equally determined to keep Yarborough pinned against the outside wall during their 200 mile per hour run along the 4,000-foot backstretch and into Turn Three for the last time.

"I knew better than to let him get underneath me," Allison said. "But when I came off Turn Two and went down to the second lane, he ran right in the back of me. Not in the side and not in the door,

Those same years of experience had taught Allison that Yarborough, a burly, no-neck, short-tempered, ex-football player from South Carolina, would no more honorably take second in the sport's most important race than he'd run from a rattlesnake.

but in the back. That knocked me sideways, and when I lifted for just a second, he went on and hit me in the left-side door and got me sideways."

Allison's version is that the second lick knocked Yarborough to the left, toward the muddy apron between the backstretch and Lake Lloyd. Both cars careened wildly along the asphalt, their drivers almost powerless to rein them in. When they hit again, Allison slid closer to the outside wall and Yarborough ever closer to the apron beside the lake.

"That's when I said to myself, 'You son of a bitch, we'll both be wide-open when we crash,' " Allison said. "And then Cale came off the infield and finally pinned me against the wall. If he hadn't hit me the second time, I would have got straight and won the race. Honestly, the only way I wasn't going to win [was] for him to crash me. I was ready, but not for where it happened. I expected we'd go through Turns Three and Four rubbing and crashing on each other. I never dreamed in God's wildest dream he'd run over me in Turn Two."

Allison's and Yarborough's race ended midway down the backstretch, when Yarborough's attempt to force his way past Allison wrecked them both. Tempers flared, and the resultant melee saw Donnie and brother Bobby Allison tackle Yarborough in the apron of Turn 3. The trio's wrestling match wasn't a stellar display of sportsmanship, but it made for great television.
AP/Wide World Photos

THE OTHER SIDE OF THE FENCE

Not surprisingly, Yarborough's version of the last lap remains dramatically different from that of Allison:

"I'd already made up two laps by running along behind Donnie, then beating him back to the flag each time the caution came out," the three-time series champion and 84-race winner said. "I had him set up to do the same thing for the win—run behind him until the last lap, then beat him back around to the flag. I had it all figured out in my mind.

"I sat there for—I don't know, maybe 30 laps—riding along in second place, just waiting. Then, on the last lap, I had him right where I wanted him. I got a good run coming off Turn Two and started going by him on the inside of the backstretch. He saw me coming and flat-out turned left, and that knocked me in the grass."

The 500 had been slowed twice by rain that afternoon, so the grassy apron along the backstretch was muddy. When Yarborough went bouncing into the muck, his left-side tires lost purchase. "When I got beside Donnie I was already in the grass and out of racing room," Yarborough said. "There wasn't anything I could do when the left-side tires hit the grass. The car just turned itself to the right, smack into Donnie, and that got us both going every-which way. I saw him coming over, but I figured he'd stop when it came to where he was running me off the race track.

"I was clearly up beside him, door to door, passing on the backstretch when he turned left. When he saw me coming on the inside, he gradually kept coming left, squeezing me into the grass. It wasn't like I'd just gotten up to him and he was trying to block me. He knew I was there and he knew I was going to pass him if he didn't do something."

Yarborough denies hitting Allison in Turn Two, as Allison has often claimed. "Heck, I wasn't even trying to pass him in Turn Two," Yarborough said, shaking his head at what he considered a silly accusation. "I didn't want to pass him until we got on the backstretch. That was my race to win, no doubt about it. I had it won, and Donnie knew it."

As their crumpled cars lay spent in the grass between Turn Three and the infield fence, Allison and Yarborough were too dazed after their high-speed melee to notice Petty, then Waltrip, then Foyt flashing past in their Oldsmobiles en route to a one-two-three finish. Allison and Yarborough were scored fourth and fifth, each one lap behind after being near the front almost all afternoon.

Petty hadn't even gotten back around to Victory Lane when the race took another bizarre turn. Bobby Allison stopped his Bud Moore-owned No. 15 Ford on the apron of Turn Three to check on his brother. One thing led to another and within moments the Allison brothers were going after Yarborough. Never one to back down from anything, Yarborough fended off the Allison's ineffective haymakers and threw some punches of his own and flailed away with

his legs. It was over almost as quickly as it had begun, but CBS had sent every historic moment of it into every nook and cranny of a spellbound United States.

From that moment on, big-time stock car racing would never be the same.

HISTORY IN THE MAKING

Most long-time NASCAR fans rank the 1979 Daytona 500 as the most important race in stock car history. It wasn't the best race, the most competitive, the fastest, or the richest. It wasn't even the best attended or the most controversial. In truth, the David Pearson-Richard Petty crash that ended the 1976 Daytona 500 was more dramatic because of who they were and the fact they crashed much closer to the finish line. (In that one, Pearson managed to nurse his battered car beneath the checkered flag at 20 miles per hour. Petty's crew pushed his the final 150 yards to finish second.)

The 1979 race overshadowed the Pearson-Petty finish on two counts: It was live on coast-to-coast television for the first time, and it featured that brief but spirited post-race fist-fight between Yarborough and the Allisons. The scuffle resembled a schoolyard tussle more than serious fisticuffs, but it added personality and human emotions to a sport that much of America was just starting to discover.

"The network's overnight ratings for the 500 were far better than anyone expected," Squier said. "Just as impressive, though, is what could be called the 'elevator reaction.' Most of what you hear in elevators on Monday mornings in New York and other big cities is about weekend sports. In New York, it might be the Knicks or the Yankees, or who won the Sunday afternoon golf tournament.

"On that Monday morning, though, the race was all you heard about. Whether it was the wreck, or the fight, or the fact that Richard had beaten Darrell down to the

> "On that Monday morning, though, the race was all you heard about. Whether it was the wreck, or the fight, or the fact that Richard had beaten Darrell down to the line, people were talking about the Daytona 500 like they usually talked about baseball or football or the NBA."—Ken Squier

line, people were talking about the Daytona 500 like they usually talked about baseball or football or the NBA. That was the first time some people in New York had ever paid attention to any race except the Indy 500. I don't think we should underestimate the important of that broadcast on NASCAR racing."

SURVEY SAYS . . .

Several years ago a major credit card company conducted a year-long poll to determine the most important moment in NASCAR's 50-year history. From an original list of 50, fans voted for one of seven specific events that helped shape and define big-time stock car racing.

The candidates were: 1) the inaugural Daytona 500 in 1959; 2) the Pearson-Petty crash that ended the 1976 Daytona 500; 3) the Allison-Yarborough crash in the 1979 Daytona 500; 4) Petty's 200th and final victory at Daytona Beach in July 1984; 5) Bill Elliott's victory in the 1985 Winston Million that got NASCAR on the cover of *Sports Illustrated*; 6) the

introduction of night racing at the Charlotte Motor Speedway in 1992; and 7) the inaugural Brickyard 400 in 1994 at the Indianapolis Motor Speedway.

Perhaps surprisingly, Petty's 200th victory won out. Granted, it was Petty and it was the victory he'd been pursuing for so long. And it was at the Daytona International Speedway and featured a fierce late-race bumping duel with Yarborough. And granted, President Ronald Reagan had flown down and was watching from Bill France Sr.'s private box, the first time a current U.S. president had attended a NASCAR race.

But most knowledgeable NASCAR-watchers argue that Petty winning a race in 1984—even with a Republican president in attendance—wasn't nearly as important to the big picture as the first live, start-to-finish telecast of the Daytona 500. "That was the day Madison Avenue first discovered racing," Squier said years later. "In many people's minds, that was the most important race in NASCAR history."

CHAPTER ONE

Early NASCAR stars Red Byron (22) and Fonty Flock (1) paced the field at what appears to be a half-mile dirt track in the late 1940s. In its early years, many of the new organization's "Strictly Stock" races were on low-maintenance dirt tracks at county fairgrounds or on tracks carved in several acres of unproductive farmland. It's been said that the Southeast's first scheduled oval-track races were among moonshiners who often gathered on Sunday afternoons far from populated areas to see just whose souped-up car was indeed the best.

THE 1940s

ABOVE: Although Bill France Sr. was quite a driver in his own right, his real expertise was in organizing and sanctioning stock car races. In the fall of 1934 he and his wife, Ann, and their infant son, Bill, moved from Washington, D.C., to Daytona Beach, where he built quite a reputation as a racer on the combination beach/highway course south of town. *Daytona Racing Archives*

The Smoke-Filled Room

It wasn't until the late 1930s that stock car racing came to life along the hard-packed sand separating the Atlantic Ocean from Daytona Beach, Florida. But for more than 30 years before, the first race for showroom-stock, street-legal, family sedans, the 20 miles of sand from Ormond Beach to Daytona Beach had hosted hundreds of internationally recognized speed trials in which men tested not only their car, but their own will and instincts for self-preservation.

It began in 1902, when automotive pioneer Ransom Olds brought his one-cylinder Pirate to Ormond Beach for several days of timed, measured-mile speed runs. While Olds was there, fellow automotive visionary Alexander Winton showed up with his Bullet and raced it along the same stretch of beach. The event, arranged and promoted by John Anderson and Joseph Price of the stately Ormond Hotel, saw Olds' Pirate reach a then-record speed of slightly more than 50 miles per hour along the beach.

Bill France Sr. (second from left) often raced against (from left) Smokey Purser, Roy Hall, and Sam Packard in the late 1930s and early to mid-1940s at Daytona Beach. France, a mechanic and filling station owner by trade, was the only driver who competed in all 16 of the stock car races contested on the beach in the years immediately preceding World War II. Apparently his rivals didn't object to the fact that France competed in the very events he helped promote and supervise. *Sam Packard collection*

The Ormond was among the finest hotel properties in Florida, and Anderson and Price arranged the mid-winter speed trials to attract additional guests. A year after the first trials, Olds and Winton returned to Ormond Beach for another series of timed runs. The fledgling Florida East Coast Automobile Association duly recorded that Winton's Bullet reached 68.690 miles per hour in smashing Olds' year-old record.

Millionaire sportsman William K. Vanderbilt came along later in 1903 and ran 92.30 miles per hour in a four-cylinder, 90-horsepower Mercedes. In 1904, during the first recognized Speed Week program, Charles Schmidt pushed his four-cylinder, 25-horsepower Packard to 77.760 miles per hour. Arthur McDonald reached 104.60 miles per hour in a 90-horsepower Napier in 1905, a record quickly bettered by H.L. Bowden's 108.59 miles per hour in an eight-cylinder, 120-horsepower Mercedes. Fred Marriott ran 127.66 miles per hour in 1906 in a Stanley Steamer with a 30-horsepower powerplant. A year later, while running an astonishing 197 miles per hour, he escaped serious injury when his car hit a patch of soft sand and flipped several times.

In 1910, Barney Oldfield drove a Blitzen Benz to 131.275 miles per hour on the beach. Sir Malcolm Campbell made his first Speed Week appearance in February 1928 with a 207 mile per hour run in his famous Bluebird. Later that year, Ray Keech drove his Triplex Special (one 12-cylinder aircraft engine ahead of the driver and two behind) to almost 208 miles per hour. That paled beside the 231.450 that Britisher Sir Henry Seagrave reached in his 925-horsepower, Irving-Napier Golden Arrow in 1929.

Seagrave's run merely inspired Campbell to run faster. The Bluebird reached 246 miles per hour in 1931, improved to almost 254 the next year, then exceeded 272 in 1933. Campbell sat out the 1934 trials, but returned in March 1935 for a 277 mile per hour effort. Six months later, after finding the once-gentle sand between Ormond Beach and Daytona Beach too rutted for sustained high-speed runs, Campbell shifted his land-speed record attempts to the Bonneville Salt Flats in Utah. As if to prove his decision correct, he made a smooth and effortless 304.311 mile per hour run there in the fall of 1936.

And just like that, the speed trials were gone. Campbell's 276.816 mile per hour

pass on March 7, 1935, in his Rolls-powered Bluebird was the last notable speed record on the beach. Left behind was a legacy of triumph and tragedy, for while hundreds of speed records were set and broken again, several lives were lost.

Frank Lockhart, champion of the 1926 Indianapolis 500 and many other races, almost drowned in the surf in February 1928. Driving a 16-cylinder Stutz-powered Black Hawk, he lost control at 200 miles per hour and crashed into the ocean. He survived the impact, but was pinned upside-down in the water when rescue workers finally reached him. Two months later, he died when a tire blew and he crashed while driving the rebuilt Black Hawk at 230 miles per hour

A year later, in 1929, Lee Bible met a similar end. He was driving the famous Triplex Special—the car Keech had man-handled to 208 miles per hour several years before—when he inexplicably lost control and began a series of tumbles and rolls. Both Bible and a nearby newsreel photographer were killed on the spot, causing racers and Speed Week organizers to wonder how much longer the beach could be used for such runs.

As fate would have it, a local auto mechanic named Bill France was anxious to keep speed-related activities alive in Day-tona Beach. Although he'd been in town barely a year, he seemed more determined than most to keep alive Daytona Beach's only real claim to fame.

Stock car racing in Daytona Beach began on the hard-packed sandy beach, then moved south of town to a course that featured a southbound portion of Highway A1A, then continued northbound up the beach. The starting times often were dictated by the ebb and flow of the tides along the Atlantic Ocean, and some races were shortened or postponed when offshore storms spawned unexpectedly high tides. Savvy drivers often steered their cars just inside the water's edge to cool their brakes during their northbound charge up the beach. *Sam Packard collection*

FRANCE COMES TO DAYTONA BEACH

One of the most popular myths surrounding the birth of stock car racing surrounds the car that allegedly left France and his family stranded near Daytona Beach. Like dozens of other tales about the man and how he got where he did, it contains a grain of truth and several bushels of fiction. As the story goes—and has for years; nobody is quite sure when it started or why—France, his wife, Anne Bledsoe France, and their infant son, William Clay France, were moving from Washington, D.C., to either Miami or Tampa (there is evidence to support both destinations). The Frances were tired of the bitter Eastern Seaboard winters, and the lure of relocating to Florida was simply too much to resist.

In the fall of 1934, with a chill already in the Washington air and $25 to his name, France loaded his wife and son and all their worldly possessions into his Hupmobile. There was nothing assured in the land south of the Potomac River except a tedious drive on two-lane highways through Virginia, the Carolinas, Georgia and Florida. Years later, when asked about quitting his job with no assurance of employment, France said the lure of working on cars in the Florida sunshine was all the inspiration he needed.

During a visit with some of Anne's relatives in New Smyrna Beach—well north of Miami and just south of Daytona Beach—the Frances agreed to stay a while. It's been suggested the decision was foist upon them because the Hupmobile would go no farther, that it had broken down and would have cost too much to repair, money France could ill-afford to spend. That's simply not true, for Bill France Sr. was a skilled mechanic with his own toolbox. He could have fixed any problem and kept going if that's what he and Anne had wanted.

Some biographers have suggested the Frances stayed put because they were broke. They use for evidence the fact that Bill France was a part-time painter until getting hired by the local Cadillac-Pontiac dealership on Main Street in Daytona Beach. Others contend the real reason he remained in the Daytona Beach area was

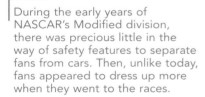

During the early years of NASCAR's Modified division, there was precious little in the way of safety features to separate fans from cars. Then, unlike today, fans appeared to dress up more when they went to the races.

his interest in the speed trials scheduled a few months later along the nearby beach. At the time, talk was that Campbell would try to drive Bluebird past the 300 mile per hour barrier during the next round of trials.

People often forget that France was a successful racer long before he became a powerful and wealthy promoter. At age 16, with his father working at the Park Savings Bank in Washington, D.C., young Bill found that running hot laps in the family's Model T on the 1 1/8th-mile, high-banked, board, Washington-Baltimore Speedway at Laurel, Maryland, was more fun than going to school. Later, using money he earned operating a neighborhood service station, he and two friends cobbled together an open-wheel, single-seat car with a canvas body and a Model T Ford engine. In it, France proved himself a skillful dirt-track racer in Maryland, Virginia, and Pennsylvania.

Given that background, it's not unreasonable to assume the likelihood of seeing Campbell run 300 miles per hour on the beach convinced France to stay in the area for the winter and spring. And although nobody could have imagined it at the time, that was among dozens of decisions that led in December of 1947 to the creation of the National Association for Stock Car Auto Racing.

But first, there was plenty of racing still to be done on the sand along Daytona Beach.

EARLY DAYTONA BEACH AUTO RACES

Shortly after Campbell moved his land-speed record campaign to Utah, several Daytona Beach citizens decided the city should continue hosting speed-related events. If not, they feared, its growing world-wide reputation would quickly fade away. Without speed, they told each other, Ormond Beach and Daytona Beach would become simply two more seaside towns with nothing to offer tourists other than the beach itself.

Enter Sig Haugdahl, an ex-racer who'd come to Daytona Beach after winning several national dirt-track titles in the Midwest. Well known by almost everyone, city officials asked if he'd create and oversee a speed-related event that might draw national attention to the area. He recommended an automobile race along an 8-mile course, half along Highway A1A and 4 miles along the beach itself. He later shortened it to 3.2 miles, a distance reached by finding the most convenient place for bulldozers to carve a south-end turn linking A1A to the beach.

The race was scheduled for March 8, 1937, around the time the annual World Speed Trials had been in previous years. It was sanctioned and observed by the prestigious and all-powerful American Automo-

No inside guard railing and only a dirt berm on the outside was typical of some tracks in the mid- to late 1940s. Cars on the infield are either awaiting another race or have dropped out of this one. *Buddy Shuman collection*

STRICTLY STOCK CARS

One of the first things Bill France did in NASCAR's formative years was insist that cars in the Strictly Stock class were just that. In fact, they were so "strictly stock" that racers and owners often drove them to the track—sometimes hauling their wife, children, and a picnic basket—then back home afterward. They were, in almost every instance, licensed and registered, street-legal, showroom-stock, fully equipped, family sedans.

France demanded it because he felt that Southern fans—and that was his primary audience at the time—preferred race cars that were similar to the street cars they could buy and drive. He knew his market, and Southerners of the late 1940s and early 1950s had virtually no interest in exotic, open-wheel, open-cockpit roadsters or Indy-type cars that were popular in other parts of the country. Many of the fans that France went after had served in World War II, and the second thing they wanted when they landed was a new car.

H.A. "Humpy" Wheeler was born, reared, and educated in the South. He got into stock car racing at an early age, covering the sport for several newspapers in South Carolina, working for Firestone in the 1960s, then becoming promoter of the Charlotte Motor Speedway. He's among the most astute historians of the sport, a keen observer of its early years, and a student of the sociological and economic forces that contributed to its foothold in the South.

"Most of the South's farm boys and textile and furniture workers had lived pretty cloistered lives before they went off to war," Wheeler said. "If they were farm families, that's all they'd ever known. If they were from cotton mill families, that's all they'd ever known. But they wanted something different when they got back from the war. The South was pretty colorless back then, and these guys wanted some excitement in their lives. And what was more exciting in the late 1940s and early 1950s than a bunch of guys coming to the county fairgrounds to race cars that looked like the ones you could buy?

"We couldn't have done what we've done unless those early race cars had looked like street cars. The big roadsters or open-wheel Indy-type cars didn't make it in the South because the fans down here couldn't relate to them. These people were into flathead Fords and Chevrolets and Oldsmobiles and Hudson Hornets. But there was still a big war from the mid-1940s into the early 1950s between stock car promoters and open-wheel promoters. Stock cars won out because there weren't enough midgets or sprint cars to go around, and the ones that were in the South were too expensive.

"Right off the bat, the other thing that worked for stock car racing was that it was still very reasonable. The cars were still something of a salvage yard product, and the parts and pieces were available and easy to find. Ralph Earnhardt once told me his entire budget in the mid-1950s was $800, and that's because the cars were virtually stock. If he needed something, he'd go to a salvage yard and buy it, then go racing. He'd just replace one worn-out or broken stock piece with another one."

Years earlier, France's position on racing by his rules was tested. It happened when Smokey Purser didn't bother to stick around for the mandatory post-race tech inspection after apparently winning the 1938 Labor Day race on the highway/beach course at Daytona Beach. Purser, a well-known local restaurateur, had taken the checkered flag and simply kept going up the beach. France and co-promoter Charlie Reese disqualified Purser on the spot and refused to back down when he and his car reappeared at the inspection station three hours later.

But there were problems with being strictly stock, not the least of which was the shortage of current-year-model cars. Because its assembly lines had been converted to aid the war effort, Detroit didn't produce many passenger cars between December 1941

> *"Ralph Earnhardt once told me his entire budget in the mid-1950s was $800, and that's because the cars were virtually stock. If he needed something, he'd go to a salvage yard and buy it, then go racing."*—
>
> Humpy Wheeler

NASCAR was founded on the belief that people wanted to see cars similar to what they drove racing out on the track. In the early days that belief was taken literally. Dick Rathmann (3) was among several drivers who enjoyed great success in Hudson Hornets in the early to mid-1950s. He won five dirt-track races in 1952, five more in 1953, then three more in 1954. He was winless in 20 starts in 1955 before going back to the Midwest and his Indy car career. *Irma Combs collection*

and August 1945. Most of the "stock cars" being raced shortly after World War II were more like Modifieds than 'Strictly Stock.' It would be several years before manufacturers caught up with the public's demand for new cars and satisfied France's idea of what a "strictly stock" race car should be.

Another of his problems concerned technical specifications. According to rules, changes were allowed only in the name of safety. Headlights were removed or taped to prevent them from shattering and littering the track. Doors were secured with a belt or rope to restrain them from flying open. Wheel covers were taken off to keep them from flying off and landing in spectator areas. Heavy-duty lug nuts were permitted to secure wheels. And heavy-duty brakes were mandatory. Everything else—from engine to drivetrain, from springs and shocks to the car's basic shape and interior—had to be factory-installed and street-legal.

Ironically, a contentious, post-race disqualification marred the first official 'Strictly Stock' race in NASCAR history. It was in June 1949 at Charlotte, North Carolina, where

Continued on next page

STRICTLY STOCK CARS

apparent winner Glenn Dunnaway and car-owner Hubert Westmoreland were disqualified for using illegal rear springs on their 1947 Ford. With Dunnaway moved to the bottom of the payoff sheet, second-place Jim Roper was declared the winner after almost all of the 15,000 fans had gone home. Westmoreland filed suit several days later, but a North Carolina judge ruled that NASCAR—similar to other sports organizations—was free to write and enforce its own rules. It was the first of several instances in the next few years that pitted France's iron-fisted rules interpretation against the drivers' never-ending search for an unfair advantage—by whatever means possible. In almost every case, France and his inspectors prevailed.

Henry Underhill and Al Crisler were among stock car racing's first tech inspectors. Crisler died in Charlotte in 1996, but Underhill talked at length in 1997 about the early days, when stock car racing was beginning to find its way.

France and Underhill met in 1949, when France flew to Charlotte, North Carolina, to have his airplane serviced. One thing led to another, and France told Underhill he might be qualified to help ensure that the new 'Strictly Stock' race cars were as close as possible to showroom-stock. Several weeks later, Underhill and Crisler were among the three dozen or so in the Streamline Hotel in Daytona Beach to hear France outline his plan to organize and supervise stock car racing in the Southeast. The next morning France asked Underhill and Crisler to draw up a set of technical inspection procedures. "We decided what we'd allow and disallow, and determined that cars should be strictly stock in every way," Underhill said. "Bill said they were supposed to be S-T-O-C-K, so we tried to make them that way. We drew up the rules, then went through and found we had to change some as the season went along."

Not surprisingly, the two tech inspectors found themselves embroiled in controversy at the first Strictly Stock race. "We had to turn away some of the cars that showed up that morning," Underhill said. "People drove up in their family sedan, came out on the track and said they wanted to race. Some of them didn't have seatbelts, and we had to turn down a new V-12 Lincoln because we couldn't get the headlights off. They weren't race cars—not by any means. They were family cars that people wanted to see run against other family cars."

A stock car from the days when "stock" was literal. With a liberal application of tape, some soaped-on numbers, and leather belts holding the doors shut, racers converted family cars into racing machines. Wally's Oldsmobile 88 was the hot setup in 1949 and 1950, mainly due to the V-8 under the hood. Wally's cooling off here, waiting to be pushed off the track. *Tom Kirkland*

He remembers clearly that Dunnaway was grinning broadly after apparently winning the 200-lap race around the 3/4-mile dirt track. "He said to me, 'I hope my customer doesn't find out about this,' " Underhill recalled Dunnaway saying. "So I said, 'That's not your car?' He said, 'No, it's a bootlegger's from up in North Wilkesboro. It was at my shop, and he told me to fix it up and make sure it would run.' "

Already suspicious because the car had handled so well in the rough and rutty turns, Underhill asked Dunnaway what he'd done to the car. When Dunnaway admitted he'd shored-up the rear springs, the inspectors had no choice but to disqualify him. "Glenn was still happy with it," Underhill recalled. "He told me he'd won the first race regardless of whether we disqualified him or not. He'd learned how to drive that way by hauling all that booze. Man, he could really handle that car."

France renamed his Strictly Stock class Grand National in 1951. Twenty years later, when it became Winston Cup, his goal remained unchanged—to race stock-appearing, American-built, two-door sedans that appealed to America's obsession with brand loyalty.

Wooden fences were no match for NASCAR's earliest cars. This late 1940s incident at an unidentified dirt track in the Southeast required extensive cleanup. It would be years before NASCAR insisted on better conditions at its member tracks, many of them little more than dirt ovals designed years earlier for horse racing. In one of the era's worst incidents, five cars crashed through the guardrail and destroyed the scoring stand at Carneige, Pennsylvania, in July 1951. Drivers Wally Campbell and Fonty Flock were injured, as was a spectator hit by flying debris. One of the cars, driven by Ralph Liquori, sailed over the railing and landed in a ditch dangerously close to the spectator area.

bile Association (AAA), the same group that today provides maps, roadside service, and guidebooks. The 78-lap, 250-mile event featured 36 street-legal, showroom-stock sedans manufactured in 1935 and 1936. In addition to a $250 sanction fee, AAA required Haugdahl to hire an automotive engineer from Detroit to certify the cars as strictly stock. The city posted a purse of $5,000, with $1,700 designated for the winner.

After several days of time trials, a 27-car grid was set that included 1934 Indianapolis 500 winner Bill Cummings, 1935 AAA dirt-track champion Doc MacKenzie, 1933 AAA Eastern champion Bob Sall, Major Goldie Gardner (a long-time friend of Sir Malcolm Campbell's), New York driver Milt Marion, and local favorite Bill France. The grid included 19 Fords, two Willys 77s, two Auburns, and one Oldsmobile, Dodge,

Daytona Beach native Marshall Teague, one of the founding officers in NASCAR, drove a Hudson Hornet in the early to mid-1950s. After winning in 1951 and 1952 on the famous beach/highway course, he was killed while testing an Indy-style open-wheel, open-cockpit car in February 1959 at the new Daytona International Speedway. *Daytona Racing Archives*

Lincoln, and Chevrolet. As close as anyone then or now could tell, every car in the field was street-legal and showroom-stock as the AAA could make them.

Few will argue that the race was an artistic disaster and a financial flop. The bumbling began early, when thousands of the estimated 20,000 fans (even then, attendance figures were prefaced by "estimated" or "approximately") slipped into the grandstands before ticket-takers arrived. The turns at each end of the course became so rutted that almost every competitor needed help getting through. (Some required getting towed out.) That led to penalties and massive scoring confusion, which only made the day that much darker. Citing dangerous track conditions, officials mercifully stopped the race after 75 laps. Marion was declared the winner, which prompted second-

place Ben Shaw and third-place Tommy Elmore to file scoring protests. Their appeals were summarily denied, and AAA declared the race official moments before officials hurriedly left town.

Stung by criticism of its role in a venture that lost $20,000, the city of Daytona Beach quickly got out of the racing business. But France and Haugdahl weren't so easily dissuaded. They convinced the local Elks Club to help them promote another race, this one over Labor Day weekend of 1937. Despite its meager $100 purse, the 16-lap race attracted 21 drivers. Even though track conditions and management were markedly better, the club claimed it lost money and wouldn't sponsor any more races. As 1937 moved toward 1938, it looked like Daytona Beach might finally lose motorsports once and for all.

Bill France Sr. (top right, hand on face) takes notes as Bill Tuthill (to France's right) presides over one of NASCAR's organizational meetings at The Streamline Hotel in Daytona Beach in December 1947. France called the meeting to assemble for the first time the various factions involved in the growing sport of stock car racing. In addition to promoters and speedway owners, the summit meeting included drivers, mechanics, team owners, representatives of automotive accessory companies, and even a lawyer. The meetings were informal and low-key, allowing guests to attend or not, depending on their interest in the subject being discussed at the time. *Tim Flock collection*

Again, France stepped into the breach. His partner this time was Charlie Reese, a well-heeled restaurateur who owned a car France often raced on the highway/beach course. Reese posted the purse. France recruited drivers and spent weeks ensuring the course would be ready for a 150-miler on July 10, 1938. That race generated a modest profit and France finished second to Danny Murphy. On Labor Day weekend a 150-mile race, won by France, made even more money. France and Reese successfully promoted three highway/beach races each in 1939, 1940, and 1941, and were planning their 1942 schedule when the Japanese attacked Pearl Harbor.

Except for occasional unsanctioned events randomly scattered during the war years, the need for rubber, fuel, and steel stopped all motorsports until the middle of 1945.

BIG BILL, THE RACER

It has been suggested that Bill France could successfully organize the Southeast's free-spirited stock car drivers because he was one of them. He raced and traveled with most of them throughout the 1930s and 1940s, and openly shared their concerns about rules, scheduling, unsavory promoters, track conditions, and safety. When he retired from driving in 1946 to concentrate on overseeing his National Championship Stock Car Circuit, his resume was impressive. He had run all 16 of the highway/beach races, the only driver to do so. He had two victories and seven other top-10 finishes in those 16 starts, and was a contender in almost every race. But he was astute enough to realize that if he had a future in motorsports, it was brighter outside the race car than in it.

His record at other tracks was almost as good. In 1940, the year he was America's unofficial national stock car champion, France won June oval-track races at Salisbury, North Carolina, and Spartanburg, South Carolina, and a highway/beach race in July in Daytona Beach. Three weeks later, after a three-day tow through the Midwest, he won a major 200-mile race at Fort Wayne, Indiana. He won a qualifier at Langhorne, Pennsylvania, then finished second in a 200-mile, AAA-sanctioned race at the famous 1-mile oval. His impressive showings outside the Southeast in 1940 lent credence to his mythical "national stock car championship."

BIG BILL, THE VISIONARY

With motorsports temporarily forgotten—after all, there was a war to win, democracy to preserve—France was hired to help build and maintain submarine-chasers at the Daytona Beach Boat Works. Within weeks of V-E and V-J Day, he quit that job to resume racing and promoting dirt-track races in Georgia and the Carolinas. In his travels, he found an abundance of local sanctioning bodies that promoted racing with maddening inconsistency. One organization's rules often conflicted with those of another organization in the next county, leaving competitors to guess what parts and pieces were legal in which event. France vowed to create a national body to not only sanction and promote races, but to unify rules, create a benefit and insurance fund, pay post-season awards based on a points system, and offer better facilities at all tracks.

Some of those ideas had come from a veteran newspaperman in what later became the hub of stock car racing. France went to Charlotte, North Carolina, in October 1945, to promote a race on the half-mile dirt track at the fairgrounds. Trolling for free publicity, he stopped by the *Charlotte Observer* to visit with sports editor Wilton Garrison. France wanted the newspaper to consider the race a national event, a request Garrison flat-out refused. As Garrison quite correctly pointed out, the drivers France expected to compete were primarily from around Charlotte and the upper reaches of neighboring South Carolina. Because of that, Garrison said, the race couldn't possibly be considered a national event.

Garrison then offered France perhaps the best advice anyone could. He explained

France realized that image was no substitute for substance, but he also realized it wouldn't hurt matters to host this all-important meeting in as classy an environment as he could find (and it didn't hurt matters that he owned the Ebony Room).

that to have a true "national stock car championship," someone (France, for example) would have to schedule a series of races in which rules and technical specifications of the cars were consistent from week to week. Points would have to be awarded based on finish positions, and purses and entries would have to be guaranteed. Garrison also counseled France to get the blessing of the competition division of the American Automobile Association, the most powerful motorsports sanctioning body in the United States.

But AAA wanted no part of France and what they considered his junk-car racing. When they summarily dismissed him in 1946, he created his own National Championship Stock Car Circuit (NCSCC) and managed it from his modest home near the Halifax River in Daytona Beach. The circuit spent most of its first year on dirt tracks in Florida, Georgia, the Carolinas, and Virginia, with an occasional race in the Northeast. Its first champion was ex-moonshiner Fonty Flock, who outscored Ed Samples, Red Byron, Buddy Shuman, and Bob Flock. To the shock of many, France kept his word by distributing $3,000 in post-season bonus awards shortly after the last race.

Bill and Anne France spent much of 1946 and 1947 overseeing their NCSCC. Despite the "national championship" in its title, the organization no more crowned a true national champion than any of the other sanctioning bodies that sprang up after World War II. So late in 1947, France chaired a meeting of drivers, fellow promoters, mechanics, lawyers, businessmen, friends, and hangers-on at the Streamline Hotel in Daytona Beach. He unveiled his master plan to bring order to stock car racing. He hammered out the concept, organi-

After spending the better part of two days in the Ebony Room atop The Streamline Hotel, NASCAR founder Bill France Sr. (in center of back row) and company hammered out the form and substance of NASCAR during December 1947 in Daytona Beach, Florida. Never one to pass up a social opportunity, France hosted the gathering in the Ebony Room, which he owned. The meetings generally began mid-morning, broke for lunch, then wrapped up in the late afternoon, just as the hotel's "Happy Hour" customers began gathering for drinks. *Sam Packard collection*

zational structure, technical and competitive guidelines, and leadership of what would grow into the world's most successful motorsports organization.

Not surprisingly—for this was his show; let nobody underestimate his force of will— France was elected president of the new NASCAR. The legendary racer "Cannonball Bill" Baker was elected national commissioner, Eddie Bland was vice-president, Bill Tuthill was secretary, and local racing legend Marshall Teague was treasurer. In February 1948, two weeks after NASCAR promoted its first race on the Daytona Beach highway/beach course, France got around to incorporating his new association.

Like every healthy newborn, NASCAR had some teething problems. It went kicking and screaming from infancy into childhood, from childhood into adolescence, and from adolescence into young adulthood. Bill and Anne France were there at every turn to guide, direct, and correct like the overly protective parents they were. They found themselves challenged by several rivals: the National Stock Car Racing Organization, the United States Stock Car Racing Association, the National Auto Racing League, and the American Stock Car Racing Association. At the time, each bragged that its No. 1 driver was the country's genuine and undisputed national champion.

In truth, there never could be one until rules, race procedures, and scoring were uniform at every track in America. And given the fierce territorialism of the day, that wasn't likely to happen without a struggle.

THE SMOKE-FILLED ROOM

It was mid-December 1947, when France decided it was high time someone brought order to the largely disorganized world of stock car racing in the Southeast. Just weeks before, up in Jacksonville, Florida, his fledgling NCSCC had completed a surprisingly successful season: witness the $3,000 in post-season bonuses and point-fund awards he had doled out to several of the organization's teams.

Now that he had everyone's attention, it was time to get down to the serious business of organizing a full-service sanctioning body. He began by inviting upwards of two dozen of his racing friends and a handful of fellow businessmen to a three-day meeting in Daytona Beach.

He called the meeting to order on December 14, in the Ebony Room atop the Streamline Hotel. (Now a youth hostel, at the time the Streamline was the tallest and finest hotel in the heart of the city.) France realized that image was no substitute for substance, but he also realized it wouldn't hurt matters to host this all-important meeting in as classy an environment as he could find. (And it didn't hurt matters that he owned the Ebony Room.)

The meetings began around mid-morning each day, recessed for lunch around noon, then ground to a halt around 4 p.m., when the hotel's guests began arriving for Happy Hour. When the gathering finally broke up on December 16, the National Association for Stock Car Auto Racing had been created. Sam Packard, 78, is one of only two men alive (the other is Raymond Parks of Atlanta) who attended every organizational session during those three days.

In the 1940s, Packard often traveled to Daytona Beach to compete in the pre-NASCAR races France promoted on the highway/beach course. He remembers well those three days in December of 1947 atop the Streamline.

"Big Bill got hold of everyone who was promoting stock car races up in Georgia and the Carolinas, and he got hold of Bill Tuthill, who was promoting races up in New York at the time," Packard said. "He reserved the Ebony Room on the top floor of the Streamline Hotel in Daytona Beach. It was one big room, like a bar or cocktail lounge. Three of us had come down from New England—me, Joe Ross, and Freddie Horton. There were some races scheduled for Florida in the winter, so we'd come for them and stayed for the meeting."

Packard recalled that while France was in charge—there was never any doubt about that—he leaned on Tuthill for many of the details of setting up the organization. Tuthill was a full-time auto-racing promoter, and an experienced and respected professional. Later, France would be called a visionary with an uncanny sense of what needed to be done. At the time, though, he was simply an ex-racer, full-time mechanic with two service stations, and relatively inexperienced racing promoter. On several occasions, he deferred to Tuthill's judgment.

"France had the idea of how he wanted things done," Packard said, "but he had to have help, and Tuthill offered that help. He kind of guided France through the start of this whole thing. That's why France brought him in from New York, because Tuthill was a professional at this business and France wasn't. Everything was conducted in a very businesslike manner. We'd have some drinks afterward and socialize, but not until the meeting was finished for the day."

Packard was delighted to see someone trying to clean up the sorry mess that stock car racing was becoming. He remembered time after time when drivers finished a hard-fought race only to realize the promoter was long-gone with the purse. "They'd be down the road, with 50 miles on us when we finished," he said. "Bill suggested that promoters deposit the purse in the bank before the race so we'd know it was there, waiting for us. That way, we'd know we weren't racing for peanuts anymore and we weren't getting robbed. All of us thought the idea of a guaranteed purse was a good one."

Packard, and all the others who attended that organizational meeting, had no idea the 1947 encounter would lead to today's NASCAR. He marvels at the modern speedways with almost unlimited seating, the multimillion dollar sponsorships, the 200 mile per hour cars, the massive media coverage, and the millions of dollars available to drivers.

"There is no way any of us at those meetings would have thought any of this could have ever happened," he said, wonder filling his voice. "When we were racing

> "There is no way any of us at those meetings would have thought any of this could have ever happened. When we were racing down on the beach, if we got a sponsor at all it might be for a couple of meals and a sign on the side of the car."—
> Sam Packard

down on the beach, if we got a sponsor at all it might be for a couple of meals and a sign on the side of the car. Up in New England, where I was from, nobody knew anything about NASCAR. Stock cars hadn't come in yet, not when we were in Daytona Beach for those meetings. There were Midgets and Roadsters up north, but I went south because I liked the idea of racing stock cars."

He drove back to Rhode Island after the meeting and talked up this new-fangled NASCAR organization for all he was worth. Later, much as France had done in the late 1930s, Packard and his family moved to Daytona Beach in 1959. "Right about when the Speedway opened just up the street," he said. "It was something to see, when they first got on that thing. In fact, all of it since that meeting has been something to see."

NASCAR'S FIRST SEASON

It took the better part of 18 months for NASCAR to begin growing into the organization France envisioned. Its 1948 season featured 48 dirt-track races for pre-World War II coupes in the Modified Stock class. Very few new sedans and convertibles were built during the war, and Detroit was still trying to catch up. With very few Strictly Stocks available to the public, and little interest in the short-lived Roadster class, France threw his full weight—for the 1948 season, at least—behind Modified Stocks.

By 1949, though, France redoubled his efforts to give the public what it wanted, and that was street-legal, showroom-stock, current-year passenger cars on ovals with clear sight lines. In February, he promoted a short exhibition race for Strictly Stocks on the 2-mile paved track near Miami. In addition to the Strictly Stocks, the card featured a 100-mile race for Grand Prix Roadsters (different from NASCAR's struggling Roadster class) and a 25-mile race for European Sports Cars. France was still evaluating his Strictly Stock class when a new rival emerged in North Carolina that forced NASCAR to get moving with the Strictly Stock class.

Olin Bruton Smith, who later would own high-profile NASCAR tracks in North

Carolina, Georgia, Tennessee, Texas, and California, had formed his own sanctioning body in the Carolinas. His National Stock Car Racing Association was pursuing many of the same drivers France wanted for NASCAR. Both men realized there probably wouldn't be room for each to succeed. As if to show he wouldn't be cowed by Smith's bombast (then, even as today), France scheduled the first-ever Strictly Stock points race for June 1949, in Smith's backyard of Charlotte, North Carolina.

It was sanctioned for 200 laps around the 3/4-mile dirt Charlotte Speedway. France posted a purse of $5,000 (with $2,000 earmarked for the winner) and set about filling a 33-car field. Bob Flock, one of three brothers on the grid, won the pole and led the first five laps in a 1946 Hudson Hornet. The 1949 Lincoln of Bill Blair led laps 6 through 150, then Jim Dunnaway led the rest of the way in a 1947 Ford. It appeared he had beaten Jim Roper by three laps, so almost everyone in the crowd of 13,000—far more than France had expected—went home that picture-perfect Sunday afternoon thinking that was the case.

But Dunnaway and car-owner Hubert Westmoreland still faced tech inspection. Several NASCAR officials had marveled at how smoothly the No. 25 Ford had handled the rutted turns, especially in the latter laps when the going was especially difficult. Tech Inspector Al Crisler discovered why: the Westmoreland-owned car had altered rear springs, a blatant violation of "Strictly Stock" rules. Dunnaway was disqualified and Roper elevated to first-place. Following him was Fonty Flock, Red Byron, Sam Rice, and Tim Flock.

Later, it was learned that Westmoreland often used the car to haul moonshine. (Tim Flock still contends the car had delivered a load the very morning of the race.) Among the tricks used by haulers to outrun G-men were custom-built rear springs that helped support the overweight trunk area. Even though there was no question that his car was illegal, Westmoreland sued NASCAR for $10,000. In words that owners, drivers, and mechanics would come to hear often in subsequent years,

a North Carolina judge ruled that the sanctioning body was free to make and enforce its rules without outside interference.

Under almost any criteria, that first Strictly Stock race was an unqualified success. A representative field of showroom stock cars (well, most were stock) had been assembled right under Smith's nose. The purse was paid as advertised and the 13,000-plus fans proved to France and his staff that Strictly Stock (later to be named Grand National, then Winston Cup) might just succeed after all. NASCAR would keep its Modified Stock and Roadster classes for the time being, but the organization was now firmly convinced that its most popular and profitable class would be Strictly Stock.

France promoted six other points-paying races that year: a 166-mile event on the beach/road course in Daytona Beach; 200-mile races at Hillsborough, North Carolina, and Langhorne, Pennsylvania; and 100-milers at Hamburg, New York; Martinsville, Virginia; near Pittsburgh, Pennsylvania; and at North Wilkesboro, North Carolina. World War II hero Red Byron, who won the

Daytona Beach and Martinsville races, was NASCAR's first Strictly Stock champion. Lee Petty, whose only victory came near Pittsburgh, was ranked second, followed by Bob Flock, the winner at Hillsborough and North Wilkesboro. Fourth-ranked Curtis Turner won at Langhorne, and fifth-ranked Jack Smith won at Hamburg.

France never worried about car count. He had a full 33-car field at Charlotte for the first race, 28 cars three weeks later in Daytona Beach, 28 cars in August at Hillsborough, then 45 cars at Langhorne the second weekend in September. Sixteen cars raced at Hamburg, 15 showed up at Martinsville, 23 at Pittsburgh, and 22 at North Wilkesboro. All told, 50 drivers ran at least one race in 1949, and 21 of them started at least half the eight races on the points schedule.

Even though troubled times were ahead, it was evident by the end of 1949 that NASCAR and its Strictly Stock division were up and running. It had been a long time coming, and would be longer still before the organization was strong and healthy enough to truly stand on its own.

Alvin Hawkins (in center, holding flags) is surrounded by drivers from a race he just flagged in the late 1940s. Third from the left in the back row is Red Byron, with Red Vogt to the right in a striped shirt. Kneeling, from left to right, is Fred Mahon, Ed Samples, Wally Marks, flagman Alvin Hawkins, Bob Flock, Buddy Shuman, Jack Ethridge, and Cannonball Brown. *Buddy Shuman collection*

CHAPTER TWO

The first Southern 500 held at Darlington Raceway marked the beginning of a new era of stock car racing. Built on little more than a hunch, the track's first race was to be an epic 500-mile battle. Qualifying took 15 days, and fans overfilled the 9,000-seat facility. Similar to races at the 2.5-mile Indianapolis Motor Speedway—the track that inspired Brasington to build in his hometown—the inaugural Southern 500 featured 75 street-legal cars in a rolling, three-wide start on Labor Day afternoon. *Tom Kirkland*

THE 1950s

Strictly Stock Makes it Big

Some of Harold Brasington's friends and neighbors must have thought he'd gone crazy. Maybe he'd been out in the hot South Carolina sun too long, or maybe he'd gotten hold of some bad collard greens. Whatever it was, a lot of people thought that ex-racer Harold Brasington had gone stark raving mad in the summer of 1949.

It seemed out of character for Brasington to embrace a silly idea like building a huge, paved, high-banked speedway for this new stock car racing series. It seemed especially silly in a backwater village like Darlington, South Carolina. The nearest major highway was 13 miles east in Florence, where two-lane U.S. Route 301 handled a fair amount of tourist traffic between New York and Florida. U.S. Route 1 was 40 miles to the northwest, taking traffic toward the state capital at Columbia.

ABOVE: Harold Brasington, the owner and brainchild behind Darlington Raceway, speaks into the microphone with his arm around race winner Johnny Mantz. Cannonball Baker stands to the right in a pith helmet. Mantz was the slowest qualifier but started 43rd because each qualifying session set specifics spots on the grid. Using heavy-duty truck tires, he simply plodded along for the first 50 laps, then led the rest of the way as rival after rival fell out with mechanical or tire problems. Amazingly, he averaged almost 2 miles per hour faster over the 500-mile race than his qualifying speed of 73.460 miles per hour. *Tom Kirkland*

Truth be told, Darlington had almost nothing going for it except its proximity to the seasonal tobacco and peanut markets of Florence, Hartsville, and Bishopville. A speedway in town? Why, ol' Harold finally had gone over the edge.

But Brasington was convinced a superspeedway would make his nondescript hometown rich and famous. He had taken note of NASCAR and realized it might just catch on. Bill France, himself an ex-driver with deep Southern roots, had promoted eight Strictly Stock races in 1949 and planned to promote twice that many in 1950. Brasington had often raced against France in the late 1930s and early 1940s, and knew him to be a principled man of his word. By the late 1940s, Brasington had quit racing in favor of farming, managing his heavy equipment business, and dreaming of owning his speedway.

The idea took root after he saw firsthand the enormous crowds at the 1948 Indianapolis 500. Later that year, during a low-stakes card game, he told friends he planned to build a similar speedway on farmland owned by a gentleman farmer named Sherman Ramsey. In the fall of 1949, after buying 70 acres of Ramsey's land, Brasington mounted a bulldozer and began shaping a 1 1/4-mile speedway west of town on land that formerly produced peanuts and cotton.

His original blueprint called for an elongated oval with each end banked and shaped the same. But Ramsey's beloved minnow pond at the west end of the property forced Brasington to accept an egg-shaped configuration. As the story goes, Ramsey sold the land with the understanding that the new track wouldn't disturb the pond where he raised his minnows. With no choice, Brasington redesigned the west end so it angled sharply away from the pond.

The eastern end was wide, sweeping, and relatively flat. The western end—thanks to the demands of the minnow pond—was narrow, tight, and steeply banked. Nobody thought much about it at the time since NASCAR's new Strictly

Stock division had never raced on a track that large. In later years, mechanics, drivers, and owners routinely questioned the sanity of anyone who would intentionally build a high-speed race track with one end so dramatically different from the other.

Brasington didn't know how many seats he needed, but he knew it would be years and years before stock car racing attracted nearly as many people as the Indianapolis 500. Darlington's population was around 9,000 at the time, so that's how many seats he ordered. He scheduled the track's first race for Labor Day weekend of 1950. He named it the Southern 500, posted a $25,000 purse, and got the blessing of both NASCAR and its rival, the Central States Racing Association.

In those days, the idea of running a 500-mile stock car race seemed preposterous to many. It had never been done. Some of Brasington's financial backers and many of his critics dismissed the idea as pure folly. But France was confident enough to give

Darlington Raceway was built in 1949 and 1950 and hosted its first 500-mile race on Labor Day of 1950. Builder Harold Brasington was inspired to the project after seeing the enormous crowds that flocked to the Indianapolis Motor Speedway. Unlike Indianapolis, which is a rectangle, Darlington is shaped more like an egg. Its west end (currently Turns 3 and 4 but designed as Turns 1 and 2) is narrow and turns abruptly. That's in marked contrast to its east end (now Turns 1 and 2, originally Turns 3 and 4), which is wider, flatter, and more sweeping. Part of the 49-year-old track's challenge is making a race car work properly at both ends of the somewhat schizophrenic track. *Darlington Raceway Photo*

Brasington his blessing and to help promote the 13th race of the 1950 Strictly Stock season. The novelty of it attracted drivers and cars not only from the Southeast, but from the Eastern Seaboard, the Northeast, and the Midwest. Qualifying for the 75-car grid was spread over 15 days, and Curtis Turner was fastest at 82.034 miles per hour. Just like they did every Memorial Day at Indianapolis, Brasington insisted the grid for his first Southern 500 be aligned in 25 rows, three cars per line.

It quickly became evident that 9,000 seats wouldn't be nearly enough. On Saturday night—almost 36 hours before the noon start on Labor Day—every motel and hotel in Darlington, Florence, Hartsville, Dillon, and Camden was jammed to overflowing. Brasington opened the raceway's vast infield to cars and trucks, thus giving 6,000 restless fans somewhere to sleep. The bad news was that it also gave them 36 hours to get thoroughly liquored up. By the noon start on Monday, more than a few of

them were too sotted to have any idea what was going on. (And, to a somewhat lesser extent, thus it remains to this day.)

It took Johnny Mantz more than six hours (at a NASCAR record 75.250 miles per hour) to drive his 1950 Plymouth the full 500 miles. The co-owners of the winning car would become famous in their own right: France, the ex-driver, ex-promoter, and full-time sanctioning body president; Hubert Westmoreland, whose car had been disqualified from the very first NASCAR Strictly Stock race in June 1949; future Hall of Fame driver Curtis Turner; and Alvin Hawkins, who became a noted promoter and long-time NASCAR official.

After the race, the top five finishers were directed to a nearby garage for a thorough inspection: Mantz's Plymouth; the 1950 Oldsmobile of runner-up Fireball Roberts; the 1950 Cadillac of third-place Red Byron; the 1950 Oldsmobile of fourth-place Bill Rexford; and the 1950 Mercury of fifth-place Chuck Mahoney. Roberts was

nine laps behind, Byron 10 behind, Rexford 15 behind, and Mahoney 19 laps behind Mantz at the end of 400 laps.

Early in the race, a crewman from Lee Petty's team asked Tech Inspector Henry Underhill to listen carefully to Mantz's car in Turns One and Two. Underhill quickly realized the Plymouth was showing too much back pressure, indicating an illegal cam. "He started pulling away from several cars that should have been more powerful, " Underhill said 47 years later. "He had more power than he needed, but there wasn't anything we could do at the time. When I told Bill France I thought Johnny had done something to the car, Bill said, 'Aw, don't be looking for things that aren't there'. . . or something like that."

Virtually everyone who finished behind Mantz thought the winning Plymouth was illegal, too. Despite the steep $500 protest fee, crewmen representing Roberts, Byron, Rexford, and Mahoney were anxious to pay their money and take a chance on what they felt was a sure thing. "The car was just sitting there, looking like a bootlegger's car," Underhill said. "When I told Bill we'd have to tear it down, he said no, not to tear the engine down. When I pointed out the illegal shocks and springs, he said we should consider them safety features."

When Underhill insisted on checking the engine in Mantz's car, France said Underhill and his fellow inspectors should examine the rest of the cars first. "I didn't leave in a huff," Underhill said, "but I was a little bit ticked off about Bill not allowing the winning car to be checked. That car belonged to NASCAR. The public didn't know it, but it did. It was toward the end of the year and I had two other jobs, so I went on and quit."

GRAND NATIONALS

If anyone had serious reservations about Brasington and his new speedway, they were convinced after the 1950 Southern 500. More than 15,000 fans had seen street-legal, show-room-stock, family cars cover 500 miles on a paved, high-banked track. It wasn't the 120,000 Brasington had seen at Indy, but it was a start.

The overwhelming success of the inaugural Southern 500 helped France strengthen his hold on Southern stock car racing. One by one, the rival organizations that had sprung up following World War II weakened, were swallowed up, or simply died off. France carried the day by repeatedly showing competitors he was as good as his word. He kept his promises to pay fair purses, maintain and enforce the rules (in most instances), and provide dates and places to race. In the end, that's all the racers of the late 1940s and early 1950s wanted in the first place.

In the early 1950s, NASCAR's reach began expanding well beyond its Southeastern roots. In 1950, when France renamed his Strictly Stock division "Grand National," 11 of its 19 races were north of the Mason-Dixon line, including stops in Pennsylvania, Ohio, New York, and Indiana. The 1951 schedule showed 20 of 41 events outside the Southeast, including races in California, Arizona, Michigan, New Jersey, and Connecticut. NASCAR made its first appearance outside the United States in 1952, when one of its 34 races was in Niagara Falls, Ontario, Canada.

And so it went throughout the organization's first full decade. It staged 37 Grand National races each in 1953 and 1954, including events in Iowa, Nebraska, and South Dakota. The 1954 schedule of 37 races included stops in Illinois, Ken-

By the mid-to late 1950s the annual NASCAR weekend in Daytona Beach, Florida, had become a huge event. Tim Flock in a Mercury convertible just left the northbound frontstretch portion of the beach/highway course en route to the southbound portion that includes Highway A1A. Flock won the 1955 and 1956 races in Chryslers owned by Carl Kiekhaefer and was disqualified after apparently winning the 1954 race.

Two-time NASCAR champion Buck Baker won this 200-lap race at the half-mile dirt Asheville-Weaverville Speedway on March 31, 1957. All told, the Charlotte, North Carolina, native won 46 races and the 1956 and 1957 Grand National (now Winston Cup) championships.

The inaugural Southern 500 of 1950 is considered one of the most important moments in NASCAR history. The top three in that first Labor Day race were (right to left) winner Johnny Mantz, third-place Red Byron, and runner-up Fireball Roberts. *Darlington Raceway*

tucky, and Arkansas, and its first road race was at the Linden (New Jersey) Airport in 1954. The schedule expanded to 45 events in 1955, then 56 and 53 races the next two seasons. The decade closed with 58 races in 1958 and 44 the next year, including a 500-mile February race and a 250-mile July race at the stunningly fast Daytona International Speedway.

For the most part, dirt ovals were the mainstay of Grand National racing throughout its first decade. The 4.1-mile beach/highway course south of Daytona Beach was an exception, being neither paved nor dirt, but a little of both. Darlington hosted the South's only paved Grand National races until 1953, when a 1-mile paved track was opened in Raleigh, North Carolina. Two years later, the half-mile Martinsville (Virginia) Speedway was converted from dirt to asphalt, making it only the third paved NASCAR track in the Southeast.

By the end of the decade, pavement was becoming more and more popular. Racing on pavement could be seen at: Weaverville, North Wilkesboro, Fayetteville, Winston-Salem, and Asheville in

Cars in the first World 600 at Charlotte Motor Speedway in the summer of 1960 wore "protective" chicken-wire fencing to keep the new asphalt from clogging radiators and breaking windshields. Joe Lee Johnson went on to win the 400-lap grind around the new 1.5-mile track.

The inaugural Southern 500 attracted a record NASCAR crowd of 25,000, many of them curious whether "Strictly Stock" cars could run 500 miles on a paved, banked track. It took 6 hours and 38 seconds (an average speed of barely 76 miles per hour) for winner Johnny Mantz to cover the distance. *Darlington Raceway*

NASCAR founder Bill France Sr. (at left, with microphone) and track builder Harold Brasington (right, in white shirt) look on as the ribbon is cut opening the 1.25-mile track. After a handful of races, the speedway in South Carolina was lengthened to 1.366 miles.

North Carolina; Nashville, Tennessee; and Manassas and Roanoke in Virginia. Paved tracks were more popular in the North. The track at Dayton, Ohio, was asphalt, as were those at Thompson, Connecticut; Old Bridge, Trenton, Linden, and Trenton in New Jersey; and near Chicago. Most of the West Coast tracks that hosted Grand National dates were paved, including Port-land, Oregon; Bremerton, Washington; and Lancaster and Riverside in California.

France saw absolutely nothing unusual in scheduling several points races in different states on the same day. On October 14, 1950, for example, the schedule showed 100-mile races at Martinsville, Virginia, and Winchester, Indiana. There were same-day NASCAR races April 29, 1951, in Mobile, Alabama, and Gardena, California. It happened again two weeks later in Phoenix, Arizona, and North Wilkes-boro. On October 14, 1951, France scheduled conflicting races in Shippensville, Pennsylvania, and Martinsville. There was method to this madness: Even though drivers couldn't possibly run more than one race a day, NASCAR could certainly deposit the sanction checks for more than one race a day.

The travel alone was enough to break many teams. The 1956 Grand National schedule showed 11 races between May 5 and May 30, all but two of them in the East. The grind began with Columbia, South Carolina, on

May 5, then proceeded like this: May 6 at Concord, North Carolina; May 10 at Greenville, South Carolina; May 12 at Hickory, North Carolina; May 13 at Hillsborough, North Carolina; May 20 at Martinsville, Virginia; May 25 at Abbottsville, Pennsylvania; May 27, conflicting races in Charlotte, North Carolina, and Portland, Oregon; May 30 for conflicting races in Eureka, California, and Syracuse, New York.

The grueling pace continued throughout the 1950s and 1960s, and didn't lessen until the schedule was dramatically reduced after the 1971 season. Other than eight races in the inaugural 1949 season and 10 the next year, NASCAR averaged almost 44 races a season during its infancy. It got worse in the 1960s: The average

Grand National schedule showed 52 dates, generally spread among 40 to 43 weeks. Teams traveled from Daytona Beach northward to Oxford, Maine; from Islip, New York, westward to Riverside, California; from Brooklyn, Michigan, southwesterly to College Station, Texas, and almost everywhere between.

This much was clear as stock car racing staggered into the 1960s: The sport had grown faster than anyone could have imagined. Tracks had sprung up all over America, each bidding for Grand National dates. There were still some minor-league sanctioning bodies loitering around, but NASCAR had clearly moved to the head of the class by surviving—indeed, thriving on almost every front—for 12 years.

This race at an unidentified southeastern dirt track in the mid-1950s features the flagman on the inside of the track rather than the outside. A Buick Roadmaster and Chrysler 300 lead the field toward Turn 1 on the green flag. By now the "new" sport of NASCAR racing had begun to take form and was developing its own personality. While not yet national heroes like major league baseball and college football stars, racers like Lee Petty, the Flock brothers, Herb Thomas, Buck Baker, Curtis Turner, Junior Johnson, and Bob Welborn were becoming more recognizable, especially in the Southeast and Mid-Atlantic States. And even though the "Grand National" division was becoming less stock and more performance oriented, NASCAR officials remained diligent in their efforts to keep their race cars as street-appearing as possible. *Buddy Shuman collection*

The legendary Ralph Earnhardt (22) and Buck Baker (300-B) lead the field to start a dirt-track race in November 1956 at Hickory, North Carolina. Several teams used protective screens to keep rocks or dirt clumps from blocking their car's radiator or breaking its windshield.

Three of NASCAR's all-time greats are poised to lap a backmarker in this 1956 race at the half-mile dirt Asheville-Weaverville Speedway. Buck Baker is in the No. 300 Chrysler, Junior Johnson in the No. 55 Pontiac, and Ralph Moody in the No. 12 Ford. Alas, they all finished well behind winner Lee Petty in his No. 42 Dodge.

While NASCAR's "Strictly Stock" series was its bread and butter throughout the 1950s, its "Modified" series remained popular at tracks that didn't get Strictly Stock events. This Modified race was at Asheville-Weaverville Speedway in 1954. It's ironic that NASCAR president Bill France didn't have much faith in Strictly Stock in the early 1950s. He thought Modifieds would be more popular since more fans drove pre-World War II cars than cars produced after the war. Modifieds were pre-World War II with almost unlimited engine and chassis changes to make them more raceable. It wasn't until the late 1970s and early 1980s that NASCAR's New England-based Modified division began phasing out its old coupes in favor of current-year-model sheet metal.

NASCAR pioneer Buddy Shuman (24) leads fellow legend Fonty Flock (1) during a Modified race on the 3/4-mile dirt track near Charlotte, North Carolina, in the early 1950s.

Ralph Earnhardt may be better known as Dale's father, but he was an outstanding racer in his own right. A terror on the Sportsman circuit, he made only a handful of Grand National (now Winston Cup) starts. Here, in No. 22, he races fellow Hall of Fame driver Buck Baker at Hickory Speedway in November 1956

Legend-in-the-making Fireball Roberts seems no worse for the wear after apparently crashing early in his career. He went on to win 34 races and became enormously popular in the 1950s and early 1960s. He died in July 1964, six weeks after suffering burns in a multicar crash at the Charlotte Motor Speedway. *Irma Combs collection*

Speedy Thompson, who went on to win 20
Grand National races, takes a break after
running a Modified race at Cleveland
County (North Carolina) Speedway in
September 1952. Many of NASCAR's top
drivers often went back to their roots for
occasional races when their Grand
National schedule permitted. *Irma Combs
collection*

CHAPTER THREE

In a tradition that didn't last long, the field for the inaugural World 600 at the Charlotte Motor Speedway was aligned three abreast for the start of the 400-lap race. Joe Lee Johnson got his only career NASCAR victory in the June 1960 race.

THE 1960s

The Most Dangerous Race Fans in America

I t's often been said the most dangerous race fans in America are three guys with 100 acres and a bulldozer. They're doubly dangerous with time on their hands, because it's almost a lead-pipe cinch they'll try to build themselves a race track for fun and profit.

ABOVE: The 1960s saw new tracks popping up around the country. With everyone and their second cousin building race tracks, things are bound to go wrong. They did just that at Talladega, when high speeds and a rough surface combined to destroy tires at an unprecedented rate.

That was never more evident than in the 1960s, when 6 of the 18 speedways that currently host Winston Cup races were built and opened for business. Two other tracks that didn't get NASCAR races until much later—the one mile warped oval near Phoenix, Arizona, and the road course at Sonoma, California—also went up in the 1960s. And as much as anything, the opening of those 8 speedways within a 10-year period offered solid evidence that Southern-style stock car racing was on its way.

From left to right, Curtis Turner, Jack Smith, and Fireball Roberts just moments before the start of the inaugural World 600 at the Charlotte Motor Speedway in June 1960.

OPPOSITE: Curtis Turner was among NASCAR's earliest stars and one of its most popular figures, at least partly due to his lavish pre- and post-race parties. He was suspended from NASCAR for much of the 1960s because of his efforts to bring the Teamsters into racing. His final victory came in the fall of 1965, shortly after his suspension was lifted by NASCAR's Bill France Sr.

For most of the 1940s and 1950s, stock car racing found a home wherever it could. Many of its earliest venues were short or mid-length dirt ovals that were part of state or county fairgrounds. Many of them were used during fair week for amateur or lower-level professional horse racing. The availability of these tracks—particularly on Sunday afternoons in the summer, when most races were held—led the property owners to welcome stock car racing with open arms. And while those dusty, dirty, rough-hewn tracks served the sport well in its infancy, it was the construction of paved superspeedways in the Southeast, East, and Midwest in the late 1960s that marked NASCAR racing's coming of age.

The 1.5-mile Charlotte Motor Speedway at Concord, North Carolina (north of Charlotte), staged its first race in June 1960. It was underfinanced from the start and struggled throughout the 1960s before emerging in the 1970s and 1980s as the unmistakable showplace of big-time stock car racing. In some ways, the Charlotte Motor Speedway is to NASCAR what the Indianapolis Motor Speedway is to Indy car racing in this country.

The 1.5-mile Atlanta International Raceway at Hampton, Georgia, opened in July 1960, then struggled for more than a decade. Series-watchers claim its adolescence was so difficult because it was built 35 miles south of downtown Atlanta in rural Henry County. They say it would have been a booming success and far more popular if

builders could have found land north of town, closer to Gainesville than to Griffin.

It was October 1965 when the one-mile North Carolina Motor Speedway (NCMS) opened midway between Rockingham and Southern Pines. Considerably east of Charlotte and south of Raleigh, it was mired in something of a no-man's land, a genteel area better known for its world-class golf courses and pricey vacation resorts. NCMS didn't begin to dig itself from its financial and physical doldrums until several major capital improvements were completed by new management in the early to mid-1990s.

Three other tracks came aboard in 1969: the 2-mile Michigan International Speedway near Jackson in June, the 1-mile Dover (Delaware) Downs International Speedway in July, and the 2.66-mile Alabama International Motor Speedway near Talladega in September.

None of them had an easy time of it. To some extent, each had financial, legal, or public relations problems, and several of them struggled through various management teams or bankruptcy protection before finding solid footing. In the end, though, each played a major role in delivering stock car racing to the next level.

THE HOUSE CURTIS AND BRUTON BUILT

Charlotte Motor Speedway (CMS) overcame a rocky beginning to become one of the most successful and innovative motorsports facilities in the country. It stands as the undisputed linchpin in Bruton Smith's ever-widening empire that includes superspeedways in Texas and Georgia, a road course in California, and a high-banked short track in Tennessee. But things weren't always so good for the track on Route 29, north of Charlotte.

Popular driver Curtis Turner was cash poor and overly optimistic when he and Smith broke ground in July 1959 for a 1.5-mile, high-banked, "quad-oval." Turner, the track's president, and Smith, its vice-president, expected the job to cost $1 million, but that was before they came up against

Curtis Turner (41) goes by Richard Petty in the 1965 fall race at the North Carolina Motor Speedway. It was the last of Turner's 18 career victories and came shortly after he was reinstated to compete after being suspended from NASCAR several years for trying to bring the Teamsters into stock car racing.

boulders to be moved, then a solid layer of granite. It didn't take long for the price to escalate to $1.5 million—and they weren't even two months into the job.

They stayed one step ahead of their creditors throughout 1959 and early 1960. But they were still more than $500,000 in debt when Turner suddenly came up with enough cash to establish an emergency escrow fund of $160,000 for the first World 600 purse. Just when the track survived that

crisis, weather and construction problems delayed its scheduled opening from Memorial Day weekend to June 19, 1960.

Even then, the asphalt was so fresh the pounding of 4,000-pound race cars peeled it up, creating huge potholes. Crews worked almost nonstop throughout the two nights preceding the first race, laying new asphalt and patching the holes. By race-day, though, most teams were so wary of the deteriorating track conditions they had rigged chicken wire to protect their grills and windshields. The 400-lap, 600-mile race that Joe Lee Johnson won was far from an artistic or financial success.

In the weeks immediately following that race, Turner reportedly borrowed $800,000 from the Teamsters Union to satisfy the creditors queuing up outside his door. In exchange, he agreed to find out how many of his fellow drivers had any interest in being represented by the Teamsters. When most of them said no, he quickly gave up what had been a half-hearted effort in the first place.

Almost a year to the day after its first race, the speedway's board of directors fired Turner and Smith, then turned around and rehired Smith as promoter.

They may have been Ford teammates, but Dick Hutcherson (29), Fred Lorenzen (28), and Curtis Turner (41) asked for and gave no quarter. Here they race three-wide in 1965 at the Charlotte Motor Speedway.

They were concerned about the pile of unpaid bills and weren't thrilled by reports that Turner was again looking to the Teamsters for financial help. Two weeks after his ouster, Turner told the Teamsters he'd actively pursue the NASCAR drivers on their behalf. He'd get $850,000 for his efforts, more than enough to bail the speedway out of its financial morass.

At NASCAR's headquarters in Daytona Beach, France's reaction was swift and predictable. He summarily suspended Turner for trying to unionize the drivers, then suspended Fireball Roberts and Tim Flock for siding with Turner. What riled France even more than union representation was the possibility the Teamsters might introduce pari-mutuel betting on stock car races. He called the union "disruptive and poisonous" and predicted that organized gambling would "spill innocent blood."

Gradually, France carried the day. He told the drivers—in no uncertain terms—that he would see to their needs and to the needs of NASCAR itself, not some huge, know-nothing, money-grubbing labor organization based in the Midwest. To show his willingness to work with the drivers, he created an advisory board made up of drivers, promoters, owners, and NASCAR officials. That convinced Roberts to quit the Federation of Professional Athletes (the front for the Teamsters), a move that returned him to France's good graces.

By September 1961, almost every driver who joined the FPA had quit and been invited to go back racing. The only two holdouts were Turner and Flock, who responded to their lifetime suspensions with lawsuits. They sought $300,000 in actual and punitive damages, arguing that Florida's right-to-work law should have pro-

Ford's "unofficial" factory line-up just before a 1965 race at the Charlotte Motor Speedway. From left to right: Dick Hutcherson, A. J. Foyt, Fred Lorenzen, Cale Yarborough, Ned Jarrett, Curtis Turner, and Junior Johnson. Team managers Ralph Moody and John Holman are on the far right.

Chicago native Fred Lorenzen came south to race in the late 1950s and quickly became one of NASCAR's most successful and popular drivers. He won 33 poles and 26 races in a career cut short by ulcers brought on by the stress of trying to be what everyone unrealistically thought he should be—virtually unbeatable in a stock car.

tected them from what (in their minds) was clearly a vindictive NASCAR. On advice of counsel, though, Turner and Flock dropped their lawsuits and went about finding other ways of making a living.

Years later, after several management changes and a brief period under federal bankruptcy protection, CMS became stock car racing's best venue. Richard Howard was one of its saviors, serving for several years as president, promoter, and general manager. During the track's darkest days, he wrote a reorganization plan that suited federal bankruptcy officials, then raised enough money to satisfy all outstanding debts.

All the while, Smith was laying low and regrouping. He made millions in various other ventures, then consolidated his power

and returned in 1975 as president and chairman of the board. He eventually bought out the remaining stockholders and got CMS listed on the New York Stock Exchange in 1995. Perhaps his best move was hiring H.A. "Humpy" Wheeler as his promoter/general manager in 1975. Wheeler is a brash and innovative promoter, a man willing to take public relations and promotional risks that always seem to work.

ATLANTA INTERNATIONAL GOES UP

In July 1960, despite fiscal problems and construction delays, Atlanta International Raceway (AIR) finally opened 35 miles south of Atlanta, near the small town of Hampton. Built and bankrolled by five

Darel Dieringer is on the pole, and
Junior Johnson is on the outside
to begin the 1965 Daytona 500.
Number four starter Fred
Lorenzen won the race, which was
stopped after 133 of its 200 laps
(332.5 miles) because of rain.

Before there were templates to follow, there was ingenuity. Junior Johnson, for example, built a Ford nicknamed the "yellow banana" for Fred Lorenzen in 1966. With its nose slanted downward, its roofline was clearly altered, and its rear deck was higher than the front. Nevertheless, it passed tech inspection and ran in the August race near Atlanta.

Atlanta-area businessmen, they broke ground in 1958 and optimistically scheduled their first race for the fall of 1959.

To almost nobody's surprise, they never came close. Rain during the winter of 1958 and the spring and summer of 1959 set the project back month after month after month. That led to one financial crisis after another, which caused all construction to stop briefly in 1959. The bad situation grew worse when several of the original investors

defected from the management team, to be replaced by four others with the administrative and financial clout to get the project moving forward again.

The track was finished by the spring of 1960. It cost $1.8 million and missed its original completion date by six months, but the huge crowd for its Dixie 300 led investors to smile for the first time in months. Art Lester, who came aboard in 1959 for the express purpose of getting AIR

through its first race, gave way to real estate magnate Nelson Weaver. Despite rain during part or all of his track's first 11 races, Weaver upgraded every part of the track and its administration until his health-related retirement in 1968.

R. Neal Batson, a member of the board of directors, was in charge of day-to-day operations when the board decided in 1969 to merge with Larry LoPatin's fledgling American Raceways organization. The lingering effects of all that rain had taken its toll, and Batson and general manager Walter Nix didn't see how AIR could continue as an independent facility. But American Raceways wasn't the answer, either, and the track was on the verge of being sold at public auction. That's when reorganization under federal bankruptcy laws—the same plan that saved Charlotte Motor Speedway—was set in place.

The track began to right itself in the late 1970s under the direction of Nix, L.G.

Darel Dieringer was among NASCAR's most popular and versatile drivers during the 1950s and 1960s. He won his first race at Riverside, California, in the fall of 1963, then one more each in 1964 and 1965. In 1966 he was victorious in three more races (including the prestigious Southern 500), with one more win coming in 1967.

Fred Lorenzen was nicknamed "The Golden Boy" when he was winning races throughout the 1960s. He came south from near Chicago in the late 1950s, then struggled in mediocre equipment for several years. He got the first of his 25 career victories in a rain-shortened race at Martinsville, Virginia, in 1961, then won superspeedway races at Darlington, South Carolina, and near Atlanta later that year. All told, 12 of his victories came on the superspeedways at Charlotte, Atlanta, Darlington, and Rockingham. He was the first driver to win more than $100,000 in a season but gave it all up in the late 1970s to make his fortune back home in real estate. He had a short-lived comeback in the early 1970s before leaving for good as one of NASCAR's most popular drivers.

DeWitt, Larry Hogan, T. Jack Black, Kathleen Nix, and Horris DeWitt. It grew and prospered. Bruton Smith bought it in 1990 and promptly improved access to and from the track, increased seating, added luxury condominiums and VIP suites, and ordered another tunnel for infield access. In 1997, amidst great hype and hoopla, he completely rebuilt the track. He converted it from a true oval to a quad-oval (identical to his Charlotte Motor Speedway and Texas Motor Speedway) and moved the frontstretch and start/finish line to the other side of the track, which had been the backstretch since 1960.

ROCKINGHAM

Just like the tracks near Charlotte and Atlanta, the North Carolina Motor Speedway (NCMS) near Rockingham struggled in its infancy. Bill Land and Harold Brasington (he of Darlington Raceway fame) had spent most of 1963 and 1964 clearing 390 acres of burned-out peach orchards, pine trees, and scrub oaks by U.S. Route 1, north of Rockingham. When they ran out of money in 1965, they turned to local attorney/farmer J. Elsie Webb, who recruited some of his business associates to help finish the job.

Webb provided some of the needed capital to continue. L.G. DeWitt also kicked in, as did J.M. Long, Dr. Bill James, R.W. Goodman, Dr. George Galloway, and E.V. and L.V. Hogan. Later, as time neared for the first scheduled race, the American 500 in October 1965, the management team of DeWitt, Webb, Galloway, and Brasington realized they had no money to pay the drivers. They each kicked in some more cash and sold additional shares of stock to raise $50,000 for the advertised purse.

The race couldn't have come at a better time. By late 1965, Chrysler Corporation and

> In the 1960s, 6 of the 18 speedways that currently host Winston Cup races were built and opened for business. As much as anything, the opening of those 8 speedways offered solid evidence that southern-style stock car racing was on its way.

NASCAR had settled their season-long feud that had kept Mopar stars Richard Petty, David Pearson, Buddy Baker, Bobby Isaac, and Jim Paschal on the sidelines. Ford would be represented at Rockingham by Cale Yarborough, Marvin Panch, Bobby Allison, Ned Jarrett, Junior Johnson, and Fred Lorenzen. The only "name" Chevrolet driver was Buck Baker, with Bobby Johns leading the meager Pontiac turnout. Fan-favorite Curtis Turner won that first race, a storybook ending to the four-year suspension Bill France had imposed after Turner tried to bring the Teamsters Union into stock car racing.

Once again—as he had earlier in NCMS's growth—DeWitt rode to the rescue. (He would rescue Atlanta International Raceway in the future.) The DeWitt family maintained control of the track until 1997, when Roger Penske bought 70 percent of the stock, most of it from DeWitt's widow, Joyce. His successful purchase kept Bruton Smith from adding NCMS to his ever-expanding portfolio, a blocking move applauded by everyone at NASCAR.

Richard Petty won 27 races in 1967, including 10 in a row, records that most NASCAR watchers agree will never be approached. Here, the seven-time series champion leads Bobby Allison in the final moments of a 500-lapper at Asheville-Weaverville Speedway. Allison made a late race pass to beat Petty, David Pearson, Dick Hutcherson, and Friday Hassler in the 250-miler at the half-mile track.

Richard Petty driving to victory at
the Carolina 500 in Rockingham,
North Carolina, on June 18, 1967.
He went on to claim his second
NASCAR championship that year.

The brothers Allison, Donnie (left)
and Bobby, in 1969. They enjoyed
great success until serious injuries
cut short their careers. Donnie,
who won 18 poles and 10 races,
was critically injured in a 1981
crash with Dick Brooks at the
Charlotte Motor Speedway.
Bobby, a 57-pole, 84-time race
winner and 1983 Winston Cup
champion, was forced to retire
after suffering life-threatening
injuries at Pocono, Pennsylvania,
in the summer of 1988. Both
remain active in NASCAR as
advisors to young drivers.

Cale Yarborough had worked a full day by the time he relaxed after winning the 1968 Southern 500 at Darlington Raceway.

The winningest drivers in the
history of the Daytona
International Speedway start 1-2
for the 1968 Daytona 500. Pole-
sitter Cale Yarborough won 8
major events at the 2.5-mile track
(including this race) and number
two starter Richard Petty won 10.

OTHER 1960S BIRTHS

Compared to the early years of Charlotte, Atlanta, and Rockingham, the new tracks at Dover, Delaware, and Brooklyn, Michigan, were glowing successes. Each overcame some minor financial problems to become popular and successful, and each has been important to NASCAR's growth— Dover because of its proximity to the major markets of Philadelphia, Washington, and Baltimore; and Michigan International Speedway (MIS) because it's so close to America's automotive center of Detroit.

Dover Downs International Speedway was built between late 1968 and early 1969 for the combined venues of horse racing and automobile racing. Trotters used a 5/8ths-mile clay oval on the infield, while stock cars raced on a 1-mile, paved, banked oval where speeds have increased from 115 miles per hour in 1969 to 155 miles per hour in 1998. The track's first advertising brochure called it "an ultra-modern, $8.6-million race plant with features unknown to track-builders of the past."

The speedway was born from an uneasy alliance between horsemen looking for more Middle Atlantic dates and stock car loyalists who believed the Northeast needed another superspeedway. Melvin Joseph, whose construction company built the track (he later became its first director of motorsports) was the most outspoken advocate for automobile racing. David Buckson, later to become Delaware's lieutenant governor and a judge, favored horse racing.

The track opened with thoroughbred races in the spring of 1969, ran its first NASCAR show in July, then hosted its first harness meet in the fall.

Dover Downs' opening stock car races— one each in 1969 and 1970—went for 300 miles. It's hosted two Winston Cup dates annually since 1971, when the race distance was increased to 500 miles. John Rollins, a wealthy businessman from Wilmington, Delaware, bought the track in 1985. Since then, it has expanded its seating capacity to almost 100,000, including spacious VIP suites. After years of struggling to maintain the asphalt surface, workers dug it up prior to the 1994 season and replaced it with concrete. The spring and fall 1998 races were reduced to 400 miles.

Michigan International

The 2-mile Michigan International Speedway (MIS) near Brooklyn was built between 1967 and the fall of 1968, when Ronnie Buckman christened it by winning a 250-mile Indy car race. Eight months later, in June 1969, NASCAR arrived for the first of its two Winston Cup races that year. The inaugural NASCAR event was scheduled for 600 miles, but shortened to 330 miles by rain and darkness. Cale Yarbor-

Richard Petty climbed out of his 1968 Plymouth to help his crew and a NASCAR official make repairs to his car's vinyl roof during the 1968 Daytona 500.

ough was the winner. After David Pearson won a 500-miler later that year, all NASCAR races became 400-mile events.

MIS was part of Larry LoPatin's short-lived American Raceways family that included tracks at College Station, Texas; Riverside, California; Atlanta, Georgia; and Trenton, New Jersey. The corporation was poorly managed and overextended. It sought protection under bankruptcy laws in 1971. It managed to maintain its race and testing schedule throughout its bankruptcy

Crew chief/engine builder Maurice Petty (left) confers with brother Richard and their father, Lee, at a NASCAR race in the late 1960s. All three tried their hand at driving, Maurice only briefly in the 1950s.

hearings, then joined the other American Raceways facilities in receivership in 1972. That opened the door for Roger Penske to step in and buy MIS in 1973. He has made it one of the best-run facilities on the CART, Indy car, and NASCAR tours.

Talladega

There never was any concern about the financial health of the track built in a place called Dry Valley, near the backwater town of Talladega, Alabama. That's because the massive Alabama International Motor Speedway was conceived, built, and paid for by NASCAR president Bill France. During his years at the helm of NASCAR, France had become a man of considerable wealth. He enjoyed substantial clout with bankers, politicians, real estate developers, automobile and accessory manufacturers, and the media.

His dream was that Talladega might someday become as important and well respected by competitors and fans as his

LeeRoy Yarbrough was a star in the 1960s and 1970s before accidents and illness contributed to his slow departure from racing. He won 11 poles and 14 races in his 198-race career.

2.5-mile track in Daytona Beach. The fact that Talladega itself didn't have anything to offer—no beach, no nearby attractions, no fine restaurants, no scenery—apparently never crossed his mind. What did was this: 1) the track was within six hours via interstate of almost 15 million potential fans, and 2) if the city of Daytona Beach ever made unreasonable tax demands, he could always threaten to take Speed Week (and its enormous economic impact on northeast Florida) to Talladega.

The new speedway was longer, wider, more steeply banked, and considerably faster than the Daytona International Speedway. It was so fast that neither Goodyear nor Firestone built a tire strong enough to hang together for more than a handful of laps. As time neared for the first Alabama 500 in the fall of 1969, that fact left many of the top drivers seriously worried. So worried, in fact, they asked France to delay the race until Firestone or Goodyear could come up with safer and better tires.

When he refused—he was, after all, the most bullheaded man in racing—many drivers loaded their equipment and pulled out late Saturday afternoon. The next day, with lighter and slower Grand American cars—from the Saturday support race—filling two dozen or so holes on the grid, the race was run without serious incident. It featured several "administrative" cautions so teams could change tires before they exploded or shredded and caused an accident.

Richard Petty, head of the short-lived Professional Drivers Association, said the dispute wasn't anything personal. "France thought the race track was safe and intended to put on a show, whether we were there or not," he said years later. "The only thing we wanted was for him to postpone the race for

Talladega was so fast that neither Goodyear nor Firestone built a tire strong enough to hang together for more than a handful of laps. As time neared for the first Alabama 500 in the fall of 1969, that fact left many of the top drivers so worried that they asked France to delay the race.

a while to give the tire companies more time to develop something safer to run. He was too stubborn to see our side and we were too smart to race on the tires they had."

Petty has always claimed that weekend's "driveout" benefited Talladega and NASCAR more than harmed it. "If we'd stayed around and run, and unless something terrible had happened, it would have been just another 500-mile race that people would have forgotten by the next weekend," he said. "As it was, Talladega got lots more attention and notoriety because so many of us went home."

NASCAR was on the verge of getting even more attention and notoriety, and it wasn't coming from anything on the track. In the early 1970s, a handful of politicians in Washington were starting to lay the legislative foundation that eventually led to a ban on all tobacco advertising on radio and television. Unwittingly, those men and women were going to have almost as much positive influence on NASCAR stock car racing as anyone except Bill France himself.

Drivers spent the better part of three days meeting with NASCAR officials discussing their safety concerns prior to the 1969 Talladega 500. All but a handful of the sport's top stars boycotted the inaugural race at the 2.66-mile track.

Pole-winner Bobby Isaac (71) was one of only a handful of "name" drivers to stay and compete in the 1969 Talladega 500. He finished fourth, a lap down, in the 188-lap race that was won by unheralded Dodge driver Richard Brickhouse.

Neither Goodyear nor Firestone had enough time to develop safe and reliable tires for the inaugural Talladega 500 in the fall of 1969. These tires shows signs of serious blistering after only a handful of laps at speeds approaching 200 miles per hour on the new 2.66-mile Alabama International Motor Speedway.

At the height of the controversy surrounding the inaugural Talladega 500, NASCAR president Bill France Sr. made a few test laps in hopes of convincing drivers to stay and race. Despite his efforts, most of the top-name stars left because they didn't feel the Goodyear and Firestone tires were capable of sustained 200-mile-per-hour laps.

OPPOSITE: Richard Brickhouse stops the No. 99 Dodge Daytona during the 1969 Talladega 500.

Richard Brickhouse became a part of history when he won the inaugural Talladega 500 in the fall of 1969 at the new Alabama International Motor Speedway. His only career NASCAR victory came after most of stock car racing's better-known drivers boycotted the race because of safety concerns.

Dodge drivers Buddy Baker
(right) and Charlie Glotzbach talk
things over during qualifying for
the fall of 1969 Winston Cup race
at the Charlotte Motor Speedway.

The opening laps of the 1969
National 500 at the Charlotte
Motor Speedway with Richard
Petty (43), Cale Yarborough (21),
and Donnie Allison (27) going for
the lead. Allison won the 500-
miler ahead of his brother, Bobby,
who's in the No. 22 Dodge.

Buddy Baker pushes a button to trigger a camera rigged in his Ray Fox-owned Dodge.

In the 1960s and late 1970s, a number of big-time road course drivers made select appearances at NASCAR events. Paul Newman is shown conferring with team owner Glen Wood. Newman never drove in a Winston Cup race but often attended events co-sanctioned by the International Motor Sports Association. Wood, one of NASCAR's 50 all-time greatest drivers, founded the Virginia-based team that has started almost 1,000 events and won 118 poles and 97 races since the mid-1950s.

CHAPTER FOUR

Richard Petty's victories brought smiles to faces all around him (not to mention making him the first NASCAR driver to earn over $1 million). The smiling man shown here is team owner Andy Granatelli, celebrating Petty's victory at the 1973 Daytona 500.

THE 1970s

NASCAR *Lights Up*

ABOVE: As NASCAR wheeled its way toward enormous popularity, Petty rolled on as the sport's main man. Shown hammering his trademark STP Dodge at Daytona in 1977, King Richard would rack up an unparalleled 200 victories (including a record 7 in the Daytona 500) and a record-tying 7 Winston Cup championships.

I n the summer of 1971, someone at the NASCAR headquarters in Daytona Beach, Florida, made a startling discovery. Stock car racing was on the verge of having its first millionaire. After two full decades of racing (the 1950s and 1960s) and parts of two others (the 1940s and the 1970s), it had finally come to this: With any kind of season at all, Richard Petty would exceed the $1 million mark in career earnings in either July or August.

Big deal, you say. Nowadays, drivers who can't get out of their own way can earn a million dollars *in a season*—and it doesn't even have to be an especially great season. There's hardly a full-time Winston Cup driver today who hasn't earned a million dollars in his career.

A NASCAR official steps lively to avoid the air hose during one of Richard Petty's pit stops during the 1970 Alabama 500 at Talladega's Alabama International Motor Speedway. Note the empty seats in the grandstands— not an easy find on the NASCAR circuit today.

Most have won several million dollars, even though they've never been consistent winners and likely never will be. While it doesn't happen often, several drivers have earned more than a million dollars *in one race.*

But riches like that were unattainable in the early 1970s, when big-time stock car racing began leaving its rowdy, unkempt, unsophisticated, dirt-trackin' days in the dust. And few things brought home the "this is a new era" message any clearer than NASCAR's million-dollar announcement at a hotel near Hartsfield Airport several days before the Dixie 500 at the Atlanta Motor Speedway. Regardless of how Petty fared in that weekend's race, his career earnings would slip into the seven-figure bracket. It had taken him 550 starts dating from July 18, 1958, to August 1, 1971, to get

there. As it was set to happen, Petty was a little put out by the whole thing.

"I've never even seen a million dollars," Petty said at the luncheon press conference several days before the 33rd race of the season. "For certain, I don't have a million dollars . . . know what I mean? It would really be something if they had a big pile of it here on this table so I'd know what it looked like. Heck, we've probably spent about all we've made just to make it . . . know what I mean? This is nice and all that, but winning a million dollars in my career doesn't mean a whole lot right now. We've still got a lot of racing to do this year."

As much as anything, that day in NASCAR history was one of the transition moments. Gone was the relaxed, fun-filled, low-pressure, everyone-help-everyone inno-

James Hylton was one of the tour's most successful "independent" drivers between the late 1960s and the late 1980s. While almost everyone has been considered an independent at one time or another, the arrival of major sponsors in the early 1980s trimmed the ranks significantly. By the second half of the decade, hardly anyone in Winston Cup was racing without a major financial commitment from someone. While few true independents lived from hand to mouth, they generally ran a conservative pace in order to save their equipment in hopes of getting to the next event.

cence that marked the early decades of stock car racing. Nobody knew it at the time, but the sport that Bill France had wet-nursed through its birth and infancy was about to grow up before his very eyes and begin cutting a mile-wide swath through professional sports.

THE TIMES THEY WERE A-CHANGIN'

You might get some argument from old-timers who still embrace the nostalgia of the 1950s and 1960s, but most serious NASCAR-watchers agree the organization and its level of competition grew and changed more dramatically between 1970 and 1979 than at any time in its 50-year history.

It was during the 1970s that Bill France Sr. stepped aside and gave the reins of NASCAR to his first-born son, William Clay France. Not only did Bill Jr. and his brother, Jim, keep their family's business on a steady course, they increased its growth rate and made it the world's most successful sanctioning body. Their vision and no-nonsense guidance helped stock car racing survive the energy crisis, satisfy the ever-increasing demands of fans and sponsors, and move into new markets. All the while, the Frances and their lieutenants tinkered with the rules just enough to aggravate everybody from time to time, and maintain a never-ending effort to keep competition as close to equal as humanly possible.

It was also during the 1970s that radio and television began making an enormous

Winged Dodge Daytonas and Plymouth Superbirds were all the rage during parts of the 1969, 1970, and 1971 NASCAR seasons. Here, Bobby Allison (22), Charlie Glotzbach (99), Buddy Baker (6), and Richard Petty (43) are near the front for the start of a 1970 race at the North Carolina Motor Speedway near Rockingham.

impact, an impact that continues to this day. Few would have dared predict in the late 1970s that within a few years every points race and most of the special events would be carried live from coast to coast and around the world. NASCAR had a hand in this, creating its Daytona Beach-based Motor Racing Network in 1971. From 25 stations carrying a handful of events, it has grown to nearly 700 stations, most of which carry every Winston Cup race and many of the lower-level Busch Series and Craftsman Truck races.

Many of the drivers and team-owners who carried the sport into the 1980s and 1990s began racing in the 1970s. At a time when NASCAR desperately needed new drivers and well-heeled owners to challenge the established stars, they began to appear from everywhere. Until then, veterans like Richard Petty, Bobby Allison, David Pearson, Cale Yarborough, Buddy Baker, and Bobby Isaac had things pretty much to themselves.

The list of 1970s newcomers who helped take stock car racing to new levels includes:

Journeyman Morgan Shepherd, who made his first Winston Cup start in 1970. Shepherd drove only a handful of races in the 1970s, choosing instead to concentrate on weekly short-track racing around his native North Carolina until going full-time into Winston Cup racing in the 1980s. Never a big winner or a weekly threat, he's nonetheless one of NASCAR's most popular and endearing personalities.

The media- and PR-savvy Darrell Waltrip came to Winston Cup from Tennessee in 1972. He brought along a portfolio bulging with accomplishments on the short tracks of Tennessee and Kentucky. He was good and he knew it, and he didn't mind telling anyone with a pen, microphone, or television camera just how good he was. But he was usually as good as his word, adding credence to the time-worn adage, 'If you can do it, it ain't braggin.'

BELOW: Buddy Baker and David Pearson dice in one of the sport's most celebrated factory battles, a high-dollar, high-stakes war between Ford's and Chrysler's aerodynamic stock cars. During the heyday of the conflict in 1969 and 1970, when Dodge Daytonas and Plymouth Superbirds went toe-to-toe with Ford Torinos and Mercury Cyclones, the two factories won every Grand National event! In 1969, the Fords and Mercurys scored 30 wins, while the Mopars won 24 races. Ford's David Pearson took home the title. In 1970, Mopar came back with a vengeance, winning 38 of 48 races and crowning Bobby Isaac as the season champ.

Bobby Isaac, who had won the 1970 NASCAR championship, tried his hand at setting several production-based land speed records at Bonneville, Utah. He drove a winged Dodge Daytona owned by insurance magnate Nord Krauskopf.

By 1971, the wings were banned, but the Mopars continued to dominate. Three-wide racing was the norm in 1971 at the Alabama International Motor Speedway at Talladega. Here Charlie Glotzbach (3) battles with Donnie Allison (21) and eventual winner Bobby Allison (12) in the August race at the 2.66-mile track.

The Ontario (California) Motor Speedway hosted nine NASCAR Winston Cup races between 1971 and 1980. Here, on the first lap of the first race, David Pearson (21), Bobby Allison (12), and Richard Petty (43) lead the pack into Turn 1.

Harry Gant was good, too, but wasn't in Waltrip's class when it came to talking and self-promoting. He ran his first Cup race in 1973, then stayed with the Late Model Sportsman series in North Carolina until finally tackling the full Winston Cup schedule in 1979. Most of his success came late in his career, shortly before he retired. That made him even more popular with the fans who'd cheered for him for years.

The area around Hueytown, Alabama, was the well-known home of Red Farmer and Bobby and Donnie Allison by the time Neil Bonnett made his first stab at Winston Cup in 1974. A high-rise steelworker by trade, he ran part of the 1974, 1975, and 1976 seasons before going full-time with owner Jim Stacy in 1977. He also drove for the Wood brothers, Junior Johnson, and Butch Mock. He grew into one of NASCAR's most popular and personable drivers. The sport, and those close to it, grieved terribly when he died in a pre-Daytona 500 crash in February 1992.

One of racing's steadiest and most consistent drivers debuted in 1975. Ricky Rudd, a former go-kart star, got his shot at stock car racing by out-performing his brother, Al, in a private test session on a Virginia short track in January 1975. He raced without distinction throughout the late 1970s before kicking off his 15-year winning streak in 1983. He won for owners Richard Childress, Bud Moore, Kenny Bernstein, and Rick Hendrick before creating his own winning team after the 1993 season.

Although success would come much later, Bill Elliott made his NASCAR debut in 1976. He and his close-knit family team (his father, George, was team owner, brother, Ernie, was the engine-builder, and brother, Dan, was a mechanic) came from the deep

Dale Earnhardt inherited Ralph's steely eyes and no-nonsense temperament, as well as his sullen will to win. Old-timers who revered "Ironheart" took to calling Dale "Ironhead," a nickname he gladly shed in the 1980s.

backwoods of north Georgia. Early on, they found the attention somewhat unsettling; after winning 40 races (all but one on super-speedways), the 1985 Winston Million, the 1988 series championship, 12 Most Popular Driver awards, and two American Driver of the Year awards, the level of fame was beyond anything the family ever imagined.

Tennessee native Sterling Marlin's debut in 1976 was almost as unnoticed as Elliott's. He ran one race that year in a car owned by his father, Coo Coo. He drove in two more Cup races in 1978 and one in 1979. He didn't try the full schedule until 1983, then had to wait until the late 1980s and early 1990s to get winning rides. He's something of a master on long, fast super-speedways: winning three times in Daytona Beach, twice at Talladega, and once at Darlington.

On the quiet end of the hype and publicity scale was Terry Labonte. Almost painfully shy, he rode in from Texas in 1978 and made an immediate impact by finishing 10th in points his rookie season of 1979. He became known for saving his equipment and becoming a factor near the end of a race, a driving style he maintains with some success to this day. His two championships were won more with guile and consistency than with blazing speed and aggressive driving.

By 1979, when Geoff Bodine ran his first Winston Cup race, there weren't any full-schedule Northern drivers on the tour. Bodine came back full-time three years later, then his brothers, Brett and Todd, joined him several years after that. Geoff is by far the most successful of the trio, winning 18 times for several owners, including himself. As if NASCAR needed any more help, it was the presence of the Bodines that opened the lucrative New England market to Winston Cup and its sponsors.

Kyle Petty ran a very limited Winston Cup schedule in 1979, the year he broke into stock car racing by winning a 200-mile ARCA race at Daytona Beach. It would be several years before he made his Winston Cup mark, not only as Lee's grandson and Richard's son, but as a confident and capable driver in his own right.

The driver who became the class of the "Class of the 1970s" was a North Carolinian almost ordained from childhood to become a championship racer. His name was Ralph Dale Earnhardt, and he followed his father, the late Ralph Earnhardt, into stock car legend.

The elder Earnhardt starred in NASCAR's lower-level Sportsman series in the 1950s and 1960s, years before radio, television, or Madison Avenue deigned to look up from its obsession with stick-and-ball sports. Ralph was a master mechanic who built and maintained his own cars, then drove them superbly on dirt bullrings where manners were checked at the gate. He was called "Ironheart" by his rivals, as much a tribute to his personality as a play on his name. Perhaps as he would have had it, Earnhardt died in his garage, taken by a heart attack while he tinkered with a carburetor.

Dale inherited Ralph's steely eyes and no-nonsense temperament, as well as his sullen will to win. Old-timers who revered "Ironheart" took to calling Dale "Ironhead," a nickname he gladly shed in the 1980s to the more market-friendly "Intimidator" nickname. They both applied since Dale raced with the same determination to win, but with more talent.

His first Winston Cup start was in 1975, two years after his father died. Dale ran just five more Cup races between 1975 and 1978, then contested the full 1979 schedule for wealthy California businessman Rod Osterlund. Together with veteran crew chief Jake Elder, the No. 2 Chevrolet team won a short-track race at Bristol, Tennessee, had 10 other top-5 finishes, and 16 other top-10s. This kid named Earnhardt, everybody agreed, is pretty good.

He won the first of his seven Winston Cups in 1980, the only driver to be Rookie of the Year and Series Champion in con-

secutive seasons. And in a symbolic passing of the torch, the first of Earnhardt's seven titles came the year after Richard Petty won the last of his seven.

TOBACCO MONEY COMES TO RACING

New drivers and teams weren't the only newsmakers during the decade of the 1970s. In Washington, heated debates surrounded whether the federal government had the right to tell adult Americans which legally manufactured products they could or could not use. Doctors and politicians had spent much of the early 1960s arguing about whether the use of tobacco products was unhealthy. Finally, spurred on by a 1965 study showing a link between cancer and smoking, the Federal Trade Commission urged Congress in 1970 to require cigarette manufacturers to affix a health warning label to each package.

In 1971, with pressure building on all sides, the television industry agreed to pull broadcast ads for tobacco products. No more catchy jingles about how good Winston tastes. No more dancing packs of Lucky Strikes. No more Marlboro man riding the range in solitary splendor, a cigarette dangling from his lips. No bellmen like Little Johnny calling for Philip Morris. Suddenly,

Bobby Allison, driving a No. 12 Chevrolet owned by Richard Howard and prepared by Junior Johnson, passes David Pearson en route to winning the 1972 Southern 500 at Darlington, South Carolina. Allison made his winning pass with just six laps remaining in the 367-lap event.

OPPOSITE: Richard Petty tops almost any list you can compile in stock car racing. Everyone knows that he has won 200 races, more than some "name" drivers have started in their Winston Cup careers. More incredible are his other list-leading stats: most races started (1,184), most top-five finishes (555), most laps completed (307,836), most races led (599), and most consecutive wins (10 in 1967). About the only category he doesn't top is the most money earned—Dale Earnhardt commands that position—but chalk that one up to racing in different eras. Long live the King; it's unlikely we'll see his equal in our lifetimes.

Bill France succeeded his father as president of NASCAR on January 11, 1972. Although generally spoken of as "Bill Junior," France was the eldest son of Bill and Ann France but was not named for his father.

tobacco companies like R.J. Reynolds in Winston-Salem, North Carolina, Philip Morris in Richmond, Virginia, and Liggitt-Meyers in Durham, North Carolina, had millions upon millions of advertising dollars with nowhere to spend them. After all, as they found out, you can spend only so much in magazine ads and on billboards.

Shortly after the television ban took effect, R.J. Reynolds Inc. (RJR) found a way to spend much of its surplus advertising budget. Rather than sponsor a single stock car team—like driver-turned-owner Junior Johnson had suggested—the company decided to underwrite the entire Grand National series. RJR and NASCAR reached their first agreement in 1970, effective for the 1971 racing season. For its part, RJR contributed $100,000 to the 1971 point fund, including $40,000 to champion Richard Petty. For its part, NASCAR was only too happy to rename its premier Grand National tour "Winston Cup Series" and its championship trophy the Winston Cup.

Compare that $100,000 total and the champion's $40,000 share to the $4 million (including the champion's $2 million cut) RJR posted toward the 1998 point fund. All told, the tobacco company has spent more than $35 million on Winston Cup racing since 1971. And it makes no apologies for its high-profile involvement in motorsports. "We have a legal product and we encourage responsible adults to use it," the late T. Wayne Robertson, president of the company's ever-growing Sports Marketing Enterprises division, often said. "We certainly don't try to convince anyone to start smoking, but we do hope to convince adults who already smoke to choose our product. We're very proud of our long-term relationship with NASCAR and we feel that in some small way, we've contributed to its growth since 1971."

David Pearson (21) dominated NASCAR races at Darlington Raceway in the 1970s. He won 5 times in the spring and 3 times in the fall during that decade. All told, he won 10 times at Darlington: those 8 plus spring victories in 1968 and 1980. Here he leads the field for the start of the 1973 spring race, which he won.

Bobby Allison (12) and Cale Yarborough (28) go door handle to door handle.

PREVIOUS: In the early 1970s, Chrysler Corporation brought these radical high-winged cars in the hopes of dominating the super-speedways. Ford responded with drop-snouted Torinos and Cyclones, prompting a manufacturer's battle known today as Aero Wars.

Country western singer Marty Robbins acquired a taste for NASCAR racing while driving in two Grand National races in 1966 and 1968. He bought his own car and drove in 33 more Grand National/Winston Cup events from 1970 to 1982. The popular driver is shown walking away from a second-lap crash at the Charlotte Motor Speedway in the fall of 1974.

Although Marty Robbins drove mainly for his own entertainment, he was a respectable driver, scoring a career-best fifth in 1974. He often played the perfect host when NASCAR visited the half-mile, high-banked paved track at Nashville, Tennessee. He was so popular and embraced by drivers and officials alike that he wasn't seriously punished for intentionally running a 1970s race at Talladega, Alabama, with a larger-than-legal carburetor.

Still, critics of the tobacco industry and meddlesome do-gooders often cry foul. They claim R.J. Reynolds uses stock car racing and its Smoking Joe's team (changed to Team Winston for the 1998 season) to promote their Winston and Winston Select brands. Which is true. They also claim the company uses its sponsorship of National Hot Rod Association drag racing and Winston-sponsored Top Fuel and Funny Car teams to advertise their products. Which is also true. What's more, critics claim, the North Carolina-based company used to promote its Camel brand by sponsoring International Motor Sports Association

sports car road racing and American Motorcyclist Association motorcycle racing. Which is also absolutely true.

From a corporate perspective, motorsports marketing is one of the few outlets R.J. Reynolds remains free to pursue. (That may change at any time because of pending legislation in Congress that would severely limit the right of tobacco companies to sponsor sports or entertainment events.) Left with few options almost 30 years ago, R.J. Reynolds studied the demographics of motorsports and found it was almost a perfect fit with the demographics of its customers.

Bobby Allison escaped injury when a hub from another car shattered his windshield during the 1978 spring race at the North Carolina Motor Speedway near Rockingham. Allison, in a Bud Moore-owned No. 15 Ford, finished second in the 500-mile race.

PREVIOUS: Benny Parsons survived a late-race battle with David Pearson to win the 1975 Daytona 500, the most important victory of his career. Despite having won the 1974 Winston Cup title for owner L. G. DeWitt, the ever-popular Parsons was uncertain of his future until he won the 500. The next year, in one of the most spectacular finishes in Daytona 500 history, he finished second when leader Richard Petty and second-running (and eventual winner) Pearson wrecked coming for the checkered flag.

Junior Johnson keeps a watchful eye on one of his cars during a 1975 race. Once called "The Last American Hero," Johnson's life has included a little of everything: farming, moonshine running (for which he did hard time in federal prison), driving race cars, working on them, and finally, owning championship teams. He won 50 races himself, then retired in the late 1960s to wrench for others. By the time he quit NASCAR altogether in the mid-1990s his cars brought home six Winston Cup Championships, three each for Cale Yarborough and Darrell Waltrip. All told, his drivers (among them: Waltrip, Yarborough, LeeRoy Yarbrough, the Allison brothers, Brett and Geoff Bodine, Bill Elliott, Sterling Marlin, Jimmy Spencer, Terry Labonte, and Charlie Glotzbach) combined to win 135 races.

Four-time Indy 500 winner A. J. Foyt was a frequent competitor in NASCAR Winston Cup racing. In more than 30 years of racing between 1963 and 1994, Foyt started 128 races, scoring 10 poles and 7 victories while finishing in the top 10 in 36 of those races.

"We asked ourselves (at R.J. Reynolds) what advertising avenues were open in non-broadcasting areas," said Ralph Seagraves, the man who officiated at the 1970 marriage of R.J. Reynolds and NASCAR, then supervised the program until his retirement in the late 1980s. "The ones open to us were newspaper, magazine, billboards, and special events. What really brought it about—just like anything we get involved in—was that we saw a need on both parts. We felt NASCAR was the type of program we needed and we felt we could make a contribution to NASCAR. I think both sides have benefited, and that's a good thing. Junior Johnson got us interested in the possibility of becoming involved with racing, but we were looking for something bigger than just one team. I guess we found it, didn't we?"

TUNIN' IN AND TURNIN' ON

The other major off-the-track development in the 1970s was the increased role television began to play. For years, ABC had offered snippets of NASCAR racing on its venerable Saturday afternoon Wide World of Sports program. But those broadcasts were edited for time, and thus offered none of the insight and expert commentary that marks most of today's broadcasts. Almost without argument, most NASCAR-watchers believe the signal moment in the NASCAR/television relationship was the CBS coverage of the 1979 Daytona 500.

At the time, NASCAR had a fairly good working relationship with ABC. (This was well before ESPN realized how important stock car racing could be to its growth. And it was well before NBC, the other "major" network, had shown any interest whatsoever in motorsports.) With little else available for live, start-to-finish sports programming on Sunday afternoons in the winter, CBS took a gamble and went to NASCAR with its bid for the 500.

Things couldn't have worked out better if the Frances and CBS sports president Neal Pilson had sat down and written the perfect script. With much of the Northeast, Midwest, and Middle Atlantic states paralyzed by an ice and snow storm, the 1979 Daytona 500 was played out before literally a captive audience. The fact that Cale Yarborough and Donnie Allison wrecked on the last lap—then fought like schoolboys on the edge of the track after the race ended—offered a memorable finish to a memorable telecast.

By the end of the 1970s, NASCAR had moved away from the dirty, dusty, and poorly lit tracks that had been so vital to its growth throughout the 1950s and 1960s. Major sponsors were everywhere, as was national radio and television coverage, and a significant increase in attention by the print media. The schedule had been cut from almost 60 races to half that, each carrying the same weight toward the championship. The presence of new teams, new drivers, and new venues, plus the solid financial backing by R.J. Reynolds Inc., was further proof that stock car racing was healthier than it had ever been.

The start of a race at Darlington Raceway is always a thrilling moment. Often called "The Lady in Black" or "Too Tough to Tame," the 48-year-old track in South Carolina has been known to reach out and destroy perfectly serviceable race cars. Or, at least, that's the version usually told by drivers who can't otherwise explain why they wrecked all by themselves. Three-time NASCAR champion David Pearson was among a handful of drivers respectful, but not afraid, of Darlington. Between 1968 and 1980 he won 12 poles and 12 races, more than anyone in track history. Dale Earnhardt also gets around Darlington pretty well, witness his 9 victories.

Dave Marcis is the only active driver to have competed in four decades of Winston Cup racing. One of several Wisconsin drivers to make a break in NASCAR, Marcis came south in 1968. He drove his own cars for several years before getting several short-lived rides with Roger Penske, then full-season rides with Nord Krauskopf, Rod Osterlund, and Rahmoc Racing. He has five Winston Cup victories: one at Martinsville, Virginia, in 1975; three in 1976, and another in a rain-shortened race at Richmond in 1982.

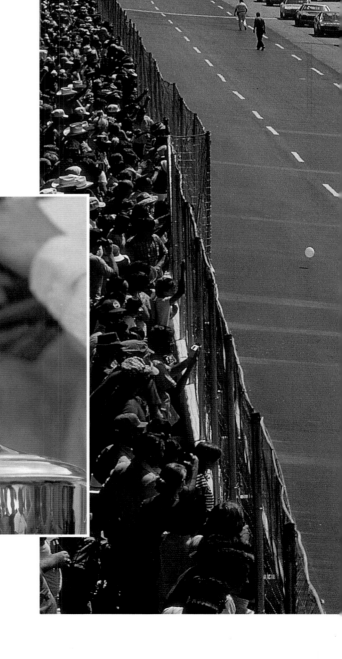

Dave Marcis drove for California businessman Rod Osterlund in 1978. The next year Dale Earnhardt drove the No. 2 car to Rookie of the Year honors and, one year later, won the 1980 Winston Cup championship for the Osterlund-owned team.

OPPOSITE BELOW: David Pearson limped into victory lane after crashing with Richard Petty in Turn 4 on the last lap of the 1976 Daytona 500.

Richard, Kyle, and Lee Petty talk racing with Donnie Allison. All told, four generations of Pettys have raced: Lee, son Richard, grandson Kyle, and great-grandson Adam, Kyle's 17-year-old son. NASCAR racing has always been a family affair: the Pettys, the Bakers, the Flocks, the Allisons, the Labontes, the Burtons, the Waltrips, the Bodines, the Wallaces, the Jarretts, the Pearsons, the Earnhardts, the Parsonses, the Panches, the Bonnetts, the Woods, the Marlins, and the Greens. Oh, yes, and the Frances.

In the early 1970s, veterans like Cale Yarborough (shown at speed in 1977) had things pretty much to themselves. When NASCAR's media exposure exploded in the middle of the decade, a plethora of eager young drivers came onto the scene, some of them with a mix of charisma, good looks, and savvy that made them media darlings. As television took over, the guard began to change.

Benny Parsons won the 1974 Winston Cup and the 1975 Daytona 500 but is perhaps better known for his radio and TV work—and for never passing up a free buffet. He's been a popular and insightful (if not oft-times overexcited) fixture for years on ESPN and frequently works for the Charlotte Motor Speedway's own Performance Racing Network. And, like so many others, he has his own radio call-in show that focuses on Winston Cup racing.

There was a time when David Pearson and the Wood Brothers seemed almost unbeatable in superspeedway races. In their years together—from 1972 until early in the 1979 season—they won 42 superspeedway events and another points race on the half-mile track at Martinsville, Virginia. Their record together shows eight victories at Michigan, six at Darlington, five each at Daytona Beach and Dover, four at Rockingham, three each near Atlanta, Charlotte, Talladega, and Riverside, and one each at Pocono and Ontario. To add insult to injury, they once won 10 consecutive poles and 12 of 14 at the Charlotte Motor Speedway (pictured below).

Buddy Baker drove an unsponsored Oldsmobile for owner M. C. Anderson in the 1978 Daytona 500. One of the first second-generation drivers to become a star, Baker was at his best on long, fast tracks like Talladega and Daytona Beach. Seventeen of his 19 career victories came on superspeedways, the other two at Martinsville, Virginia, and Nashville, Tennessee. He drove for some of the best teams in NASCAR: Cotton Owens, Petty Enterprises, Nord Krauskopf, Bud Moore, Harry Ranier, and the Wood Brothers. He retired in the early 1990s and has done well as a TV commentator.

Richard Petty at speed at the 1979 Daytona 500. It was one of the most improbable finishes in Winston Cup history.

Donnie Allison was leading the 1979 Daytona 500 for owner Hoss Ellington until a last-lap crash with Cale Yarborough.

Donnie Allison pits during the 1979 Daytona 500. The pit crew did everything they could do, but to no avail.

CHAPTER FIVE

When you talk about the 1980s, one name comes to the forefront: Dale Earnhardt. The "Intimidator" picked up where Petty left off, cranking out titles with steady driving and a knack for squeezing 2 yards of car through 5 feet of space.

THE 19 80s

Corporate America Goes Racin'

There is a story about how Buddy Baker decided to become an owner/driver. This was in 1984, and Baker was a reputable contract driver. But Baker reasoned that drivers are expendable. But a good owner—and he fancied himself as good owner material— would never fire a good driver. Which, of course, he also fancied himself. So it was that Baker and business partner Danny Schiff created Baker/Schiff Racing, leased a shop, started building some Oldsmobiles, and got Crisco backing for 1985.

ABOVE: Earnhardt spent the better part of the 1980 season in victory lane, pulling down 5 wins and an amazing 24 top-ten finishes on his way to his first Winston Cup Championship.

Things were just peachy until Baker visited a nearby machine shop to see about some cylinder head work and to pick up some valves. The counterman said the bill was "fifty-five eighty," and Baker was delighted the tab wasn't going to break him. He pulled out a hundred dollar bill and waited for change, only to bump head-on into the harsh truth about racing.

Benny Parsons was one of
NASCAR's most articulate and
popular spokesmen throughout
his 25-year career. In a career that
stretched from 1964 to 1988,
Parsons took home 21 Winston
Cup/Grand National victories.
Among his career highlights were
the 1973 Winston Cup
championship and the 1975
Daytona 500 trophy.

"I knew I was in deep trouble," he said years later, "when the guy said he meant $5,580, not $55.80. I thought, 'Oh, Lord, what have I got myself into now?' "

The cost of doing business was one of several dramatic changes that emerged in the 1980s. Compared to the explosive growth from 1980 through 1989, the previous 30 years had been positively primitive. Almost everything about stock car racing changed in the 1980s: its personalities and venues, the equipment, its standing within the media community, and its growing acceptance from an American public that seemed disenchanted with traditional major league sports that continued to deliver far less than promised.

That said, it should be noted that nothing changed more in the 1980s than the finances required to keep a competitive car on the track. And within that general framework, nothing changed more than the level of involvement from corporate America. For that, today's owners, drivers, crew chiefs, crewmen, and fans can thank television in general, and ESPN in particular. (Baker, by the way, got rid of his team in the early 1990s in favor of a radio/television career with several networks.)

It's generally accepted that the 1979 Daytona 500 was the single most important event in the history of NASCAR racing. It featured an exciting and controversial finish to the sport's most important event, a race delivered live from start to finish into tens of millions of homes via CBS television. As if by magic (which, as everyone knows, usually comes disguised as hard work), the sport that had labored for so long as a regional pastime began building its national constituency thanks to the country's growing infatuation with cable television.

At the time, the three major over-the-air networks had little use for motorsports. Granted, CBS had done the historic 1979 Daytona 500 live from start to finish, but the primary Sunday afternoon offerings from the Big Three were more mainstream: the National Football League in the fall, professional golf in the spring and summer, the occasional major tennis tournament, and key NCAA and NBA games. There was a time when the Tour de France bicycle race got more air time than major motorsports. And also fighting for TV time were figure skating, gymnastics, boxing, snow skiing, and the occasional soccer game.

In truth, motorsports' demographics weren't the most appealing to advertisers. That's because most races were run in fairly small markets where the overnight ratings barely made a blip on the Nielson Ratings. The perception (the misconception, as it turned out) was that racing appealed primarily to undereducated, lower- to middle-class white males with blue-collar jobs, and hardly any sophistication. And that didn't exactly send shivers of anticipation through the suits on Madison Avenue and Wall Street.

But the fledgling cable network industry took an altogether different view. Since they were the new kids on the block, they were perfectly willing to work harder and take more chances to make themselves accepted as part of the neighborhood. They eagerly jumped into the fray and offered to televise

Buddy Baker pulled out a hundred dollar bill and waited for change, only to bump head-on into the harsh truth about racing. "I knew I was in deep trouble," he said years later, "when the guy said he meant $5,580, not $55.80. I thought, 'Oh, Lord, what have I got myself into now?'"

the races that CBS and NBC and ABC chose to ignore—which was just about everything other than the Daytona 500. Rather than as a dead-end street, the fledgling Entertainment and Sports Programming Network (ESPN) of Bristol, Connecticut, looked at racing in general, and NASCAR in particular, as a superhighway into the homes of millions of new viewers.

Many NASCAR-watchers believe the exposure offered by ESPN (and later, The Nashville Network (TNN), WTBS, and ESPN2) proved more valuable than anything offered by weekly magazines, trade papers, and the mainstream media combined. For the first time, loyal fans and those becoming fans had access to live races from tracks the networks ignored. The networks could hardly be blamed. What was CBS to do, drop The Masters for a 400-lap race at North Wilkesboro, North Carolina, or ignore the U.S. Open Tennis Championships for a short-track race from Richmond, Virginia?

ESPN's contributions weren't lost on the men who arguably would benefit the most, the drivers. "Much of the credit for this sport's growing audience and active involvement by big-name corporate sponsors must go to ESPN," said seven-time NASCAR champion Dale Earnhardt. "It's been great for us. The more television has covered our races—bringing in new sponsors with it—the more it has contributed to our growth. It certainly has gotten us out to the fans."

The upstart "cable guy" wasn't too proud to negotiate deals for rights to races ignored by the major networks. ESPN's first Winston Cup broadcast was from the North Carolina Motor Speedway in March 1981, a 500-miler it taped for replay several days later. Its first live, start-to-finish offering

Pole-sitter Buddy Baker went on to win the 1980 Daytona 500 for owner Harry Ranier. Three years later Baker won the midsummer Firecracker 400 for the Wood Brothers.

came in November 1981, from the Atlanta Motor Speedway. It presented eight live Winston Cup broadcasts in 1982, five live and one tape-delayed the next year, then seven live broadcasts in 1984. It showcased a total of 59 live broadcasts the rest of the 1980s, going from 13 to 9, back to 13, and then 17, before broadcasting 20 Winston Cup races live in 1989.

Al Robinson, director of media and marketing at Dover Downs International Speedway, was watching carefully as ESPN began stretching its legs in the early 1980s. He remembers its pioneering spirit and its impact on corporate America. "It was a case of the network looking for sports programming and NASCAR looking for a carrier to get more exposure," he said. "The development of the cable industry and the numbers of homes that signed on throughout the 1980s was crucial to how NASCAR grew.

"If stock car coverage had been limited to just the three over-air networks, I doubt we'd have every event on television like we do today," he said. "For sure, I don't think we'd have every event live from start to finish. It might be that most races would be covered like a professional golf tournament, with the network coming on with two hours to go and staying with the race to the end. No question, the cable industry changed the way television does stock car racing."

Inexorably, the emergence of cable television began a cycle that continues to this day. ESPN and its latter-day cousins helped cultivate new fans in parts of America that had only a vague understanding and appreciation of Winston Cup racing. That ever-growing fan base and the increased television ratings caught the attention of several Fortune 500 companies. Their presence as major sponsors helped bring several new teams into Winston Cup. More teams and more new drivers created new rivalries, which attracted even more fans. As the cycle came full circle, speedway operators

Bobby Allison enjoyed great success in the Gatorade-sponsored cars owned by the potent DiGard team. The decade of the 1980s offered the best and worst of racing for the Florida native and long-time Alabama resident. He got 22 of his 83 career victories in the 1980s (driving for Bud Moore, DiGard, and the Stavola brothers) and won the 1983 Winston Cup. He was at the top of his game when a frightening accident at Pocono, Pennsylvania, in the summer of 1988 ended his career. His final victory came earlier that year in the 1988 Daytona 500, where he beat his son Davey in a stirring last-lap duel.

The Junior Johnson team gives Darrell Waltrip quick service en route to their victory in the 1981 spring race at Darlington Raceway.

were forced to upgrade their facilities and add seats. And it caused them to also improve and expand the areas where the radio and television people plied their trade.

All of which directly led to an increase in sponsorship money.

As 1979 turned into 1980, all but a handful of the sponsors of major, full-schedule NASCAR teams were local or regional. STP with Richard Petty was an exception. So were Busch with Cale Yarborough, Gatorade with Darrell Waltrip, and Purolator with Neil Bonnett. The Pepsi-Cola Co. came aboard in 1981 with Waltrip (Gatorade stayed in the sport with Ricky Rudd), as did Valvoline with Yarborough, Skoal with Harry Gant, Hardee's with

Bobby Allison, and Wrangler with Dale Earnhardt. Busch stayed in NASCAR as sponsor of the annual Busch Clash and was the "official" beer of the organization.

In 1982, new sponsors included Piedmont Airlines with Rudd, 7-Eleven with Gant, and Levi Garrett with Morgan Shepherd. Additional brewing companies emerged in 1983: Miller High Life sponsored Allison, Budweiser came in with Terry Labonte, and Old Milwaukee with ex-Indy car driver Tim Richmond. The 1984 season saw Coors replace Melling Tool for driver Bill Elliott, and Budweiser double its involvement by sponsoring a second Junior Johnson-owned team for Bonnett. And for the first time, a Charlotte, North Carolina,

BELOW: Long-time Sportsman and Late Model favorite Harry Gant worked his way from weekly short-track racing in the Southeast to become one of NASCAR's most popular Winston Cup stars in the 1980s and 1990s. He found more success late in his career when he became the Skoal Bandit driver for Hollywood stuntman Hal Needham and movie star Burt Reynolds.

BOTTOM: Harry Gant awaits his turn to qualify at Darlington Raceway in 1982. Gant came to full-time Winston Cup racing late in his career but still managed to win 17 poles, 18 races, and millions of fans.

Ricky Rudd has won races for team owners Richard Childress, Bud Moore, Kenny Bernstein, Rick Hendrick, and his own North Carolina-based RMP team. Unlike most modern-day NASCAR stars, Rudd didn't come into Winston Cup after years of weekly, short-track racing. He was an outstanding go-kart racer and came to stock cars directly from that discipline while still in high school. Among his 19 career victories are 5 on road courses, 3 on short tracks, and 11 on speedways: 1 each at Michigan, Darlington, Rockingham, Atlanta, Phoenix, Loudon, and Indianapolis, and 4 at Dover.

businessman, Rick Hendrick, unveiled a Chevrolet team for Geoff Bodine. It started as All-Star Racing, but picked up backing midway through the season from Northwestern Security Insurance Co.

By now, the pattern was clear: The cost of going racing was forcing all but the strongest and most resilient sponsors to the sidelines. Full-season sponsorships that once cost less than $200,000 were up to $450,000 by the early 1980s. They began reaching the $1-million mark in the late-1980s, followed by a steady climb toward today's full-schedule sponsorship packages of between $4 mil-

lion and $6 million. But instead of losing teams and offering an inferior product, NASCAR gained stronger and better-financed teams with owners and drivers committed to moving ahead with the times.

Among them: the GM Goodwrench division of General Motors with the Childress/Earnhardt team; Folgers coffee with Hendrick/Ken Schrader; Zerex with a young Wisconsin owner/driver named Alan Kulwicki; the Havoline division of Texaco with Robert Yates and second-generation driver Davey Allison; the Motorcraft division of Ford Motor Co. with owner Bud Moore and driver Brett Bodine; the film division of Eastman Kodak with the Morgan-McClure team featuring Rick Wilson; Kodiak smokeless tobacco with owner Raymond Beadle

and Rusty Wallace; second-generation driver Sterling Marlin with owner Billy Hagan and Sunoco; Stroh's beer with owner Jack Roush and driver Mark Martin; and Proctor and Gamble's Tide detergent with Hendrick and Waltrip.

More than just money—as if that wasn't important enough—the influx of major sponsors confirmed that NASCAR had grown beyond its local and regional bounds. Consider the image and prestige conveyed by the presence of Ford, General Motors, Quaker State, Pepsi-Cola, Budweiser, Tide, Piedmont Airlines, the South-

Nobody knew it at the time. Indeed, how could they have imagined such a thing? But Richard Petty's July 1984 victory in the Pepsi 400 at Daytona International Speedway was the last of his record-setting 200. He finally retired after the 1992 season.

Ricky Rudd drove for driver-turned-owner Richard Childress in 1982 and 1983, winning for the team at Riverside, California, and Martinsville, Virginia, in 1983. Rudd was the first full-schedule Richard Childress Racing driver and was succeeded in the No. 3 cars by Dale Earnhardt. Ironically, Rudd went from Childress to Bud Moore when Earnhardt left Moore to come to Childress.

land Corporation, Valvoline, Gatorade, and Miller. Compare that to some of sponsors in the early 1980s: Tri-City Aluminum, Belden Asphalt, Barnes Freight Lines, Bo Law Automotive, South Hill Texaco, Stone's Cafeteria, King's Mountain Truck Stop, Bluegrass Express, Iron Peddler, Wooten's Texaco, and Reid Trailer Sales.

By 1989, every major full-schedule team was sponsored by at least one corporation that marketed itself through stock car racing. Wallace, the champion, with Kodiak. Runner-up Earnhardt with GM Goodwrench, third-place Martin by Stroh's,

fourth-place Waltrip by Tide, and fifth-place Ken Schrader by Folgers. Among the other major sponsors as the decade ended: Levi Garrett, Peak, Valvoline, Citgo, Purolator, Zerex, Quaker State, Hardee's, Texaco Havoline, Crisco, Heinz 57, Coors, County Time, Winn-Dixie, and Budweiser.

TRACK GROWTH
AND RENEWAL

Paralleling the economic health of Winston Cup racing was the dramatic improvements in its venues. The antiquated (downtrodden, some called it) half-mile State

Shortly after Ronald Reagan gave the command, "Gentlemen, start your engines," while en route to the race in Air Force One, Petty started sixth for his 200th victory at the 1984 Pepsi 400 and beat out pole-sitter Cale Yarborough to the flag. Harry Gant finished second when Yarborough pulled off into pit lane a lap early. Dale Earnhardt's eighth-place finish put him into the points lead for a while, which he would surrender to Terry Labonte a few weeks later at Bristol. Labonte went on to win the 1984 title.

Bill Elliott collected the inaugural Winston Million with a dramatic victory in the Labor Day weekend 1985 Southern 500 at Darlington Raceway.

Fairgrounds Raceway in Richmond, Virginia, was renovated into a clean and modernistic 3/4-mile, D-shaped track. It sported 65,000 seats (more than twice the old track's capacity) and was equipped with skyboxes, VIP suites, pedestrian and vehicles tunnels for improved traffic flow, and immaculate landscaping. The work was completed between February and September of 1988, an amazing accomplishment given the amount of demolition and site preparation needed. Within two years, the renamed Richmond International Raceway had lights, and its two sold-out races had been moved to prime time on Saturday nights in June and September.

The Charlotte Motor Speedway underwent major renovations throughout the 1980s. Seating was expanded from 75,000 to almost 100,000, making it one of NASCAR's largest facilities. An on-site business complex was built, along with an exclusive restaurant and night club that overlooks the frontstretch. High-rise condominiums were built in Turn One, affording residents and their guests one of the best views in all of motorsports.

Because of the speedway's facilities and locale within the heart of stock car country, R.J. Reynolds and NASCAR named CMS to host the inaugural Winston all-star race in 1985. Named for RJR's flagship cigarette brand, the race was limited to drivers who had won a points-paying race the previous season. It offered a $320,000 purse for the 12 drivers in the 70-lap race, which Darrell Waltrip won with an engine that (ahem!) erupted so thoroughly after taking the checkered flag there was hardly enough left for officials to inspect.

Additional seating, upgraded driver and crew facilities, and luxury skyboxes for corporate VIPs and sponsors began appearing at almost every track. After a 19-year absence, NASCAR returned to the famous Watkins Glen (New York) International road course with a Winston Cup race in 1986. Two years later teams visited the 1-mile Phoenix International Raceway for the first time, then went to the 2.52-mile road course at Sonoma, California, the next year. On the negative side: the 2.5-mile Ontario (California) Motor Speedway closed after the 1980 season; the 2-mile track at College Station, Texas, ran its last NASCAR race in 1981; the half-mile Nashville (Tennessee) Raceway hosted its final Cup race in 1984; and the 2.62-mile Riverside (California) Raceway shut down after the 1988 Winston Cup season.

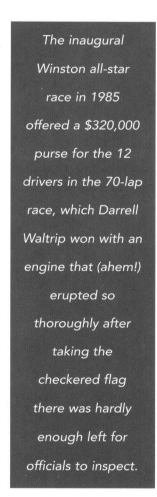

The inaugural Winston all-star race in 1985 offered a $320,000 purse for the 12 drivers in the 70-lap race, which Darrell Waltrip won with an engine that (ahem!) erupted so thoroughly after taking the checkered flag there was hardly enough left for officials to inspect.

THE HEROES SHINE ON

Many of the sport's biggest names enjoyed some of their greatest moments in the 1980s. Darrell Waltrip won his three championships with Junior Johnson and captured 57 of his 84 career victories in that decade with DiGard, Johnson, and Hendrick Motorsports. After being Rookie of the Year the previous season, Dale Earnhardt won the first of his seven NASCAR championships in 1980, added titles in 1986 and 1987, and won 38 races for Rod Osterlund, Bud Moore, and Richard Childress during the 1980s.

After being runner-up five times and wondering if he'd ever finish any higher, Bobby Allison won the 1983 NASCAR championship. Terry Labonte got the first of his two titles in 1984, then a couple of up-and-coming drivers named Bill Elliott and Rusty Wallace won championships in 1988 and 1989, respectively. Elliott also won the inaugural Winston Million in 1985, taking a $1 million payday for winning the Daytona 500 in Daytona Beach, the Winston

Why does stock car racing work? What is it about street-appearing cars running in circles that attracts blue-collar, workaday fans to the same event that has attracted doctors, lawyers, corporate CEOs, and middle-class businessmen? Why is stock car racing in general, and NASCAR Winston Cup racing in particular, so much more popular than any other form of motorsports in America? (The Indianapolis 500 is the once-a-year exception.)

Some of the toughest tickets in American sports are for the annual races in Daytona Beach, Richmond, Loudon, Dover, at Indianapolis in August, and at Martinsville and Bristol. Despite adding seats almost annually, speedways are selling out earlier than ever. Several tracks have lengthy waiting lists of fans hoping for a chance at whatever season tickets might not be renewed in time.

Ratings are at an all-time high now that every race—and many qualifying sessions—is being televised. There are a handful of weekly television shows that focus exclusively on NASCAR, and several others that pay major attention to Winston Cup, Busch Series, and Craftsman Truck racing. And you can't turn around in a bookstore these days without bumping into yet another NASCAR-related book or magazine.

Men, women, and children of all ages, races, and economic stations embrace stock car racing. *Sports Illustrated* has called it America's fastest growing sport, and drivers have appeared on the cover of everything from *SI* to *TV Guide* to *People* to *Inside Sports*. ESPN, ESPN2, The Nashville Network, WTBS, and the A&E Network have devoted hours of time to racing and its star drivers and owners.

An Industry Insider's Take

Tom Cotter has been around the sport for a dozen years, many of them as head of his own motorsports-related marketing and public relations firm in the shadow of the Charlotte Motor Speedway. This is why he thinks it works:

"You've got 32 races a year, and that's a lot more than IndyCar and drag racing or Formula 1. It's almost like a soap opera or a serial played out almost every weekend—almost like *Knots Landing* or *Days of Our Lives*. All these different scenarios playing out on the race track almost every weekend. There are 42 different stories every weekend, and the fans can't wait to see what happens in the next episode.

"And in the middle of those episodes, it's like reading Soap Opera Digest. There are things happening in the background: drivers coming, drivers going, crew chiefs coming and going, sponsorship changes. People get so wrapped up in the episodes that the sport takes on a life of its own.

"It started taking off maybe a decade ago, but it's like a snowball rolling down a hill. Little by little, stock car racing has been picking up momentum, getting bigger and bigger. Until maybe 10 years ago, I think the rest of the country thought it was just a redneck, Southern sport, something that hillbillies liked. People outside the sport began realizing it was something special with great entertainment value when some national publications began paying attention.

"In the early days, going back maybe 10 years, the corporations involved wanted exposure on TV. It was just this thing that people within the company knew had some value, but they really weren't sure how much value, and they were very unsure of how to measure it. It was so hard to say, 'We ran a race in Charlotte and the car ran well,' but did that actually translate into sales? But as racing has become a bigger-league player, you don't have to explain to CEOs and company presidents what NASCAR is. As racing has become a bigger player in the world of entertainment and sponsorship, people with a lot of money to invest—in football programs or golf or the NCAA or tennis or hockey—are finding that stock car racing is coming into their business lives.

"Now, you have people with MBAs—people making major business decisions—with a very high level of awareness in stock car racing. I've yet to meet a company person who didn't say they didn't need to win a race, then turn around and be upset that they didn't win.

"I don't see any end to it. There are more big companies that want to get into quality programs than there are quality programs available. I see companies that can't afford to pay for Winston Cup getting into Busch Grand National or the Craftsman Truck series. They can do that for 20 or 25 percent less money, and get a lot of exposure. Not as much as in Cup, but good exposure for what they're spending.

"What does it cost? A back-of-the-pack to middle-of-the-pack team will cost about $4 million. There are some out there for $6 to $6.5 million, and that's what it'll cost if you want to be a top-10 team. But the top-10 teams are pretty much sewed up for years with sponsors, and if you give that kind of money to a middle- or back-of-the pack team, it doesn't mean you'll suddenly have a top-10 team.

"One of the most important moments was when Tide came in for the 1987 season. It was the first non-male, non-beer, non-tobacco, non-automotive consumer product company to come into the sport and do it big-time. They had a big show-car program, a big staff, a big advertising campaign, terrific on-package racing graphics. They were the first ones to put racing on the package. Other consumer products companies had been in racing before, but they didn't do it like Tide did it. And they didn't stay in it very long.

"The next wave will be business to business. A Bill Gates putting on a big marketing program, and inviting the CEO of General Motors to a stock car race and showing him a good time. Then that guy goes back and buys a wad of Gates' products. It won't necessarily be win on Sunday and sell on Monday. It'll be more like one company entertaining another company, with not as much individual customer sales involved."

The key to NASCAR's popularity is something everyone from marketing executives to sports promoters would like to uncover. "People like to see people doing dangerous things," says Humpy Wheeler. "What we have to be careful about is to keep the sawdust in it." Wheeler keeps the fans packing the Charlotte Motor Speedway stands with events like The Winston, an invitation-only all-star race. The shot above is from the 1992 running of the event.

WHY IS STOCK CAR RACING SO POPULAR?

What Humpy Thinks

H. A. "Humpy" Wheeler has been around racing almost all his life. Born in North Carolina and educated in South Carolina, he wrote about the early years of stock car racing, worked for Firestone when it was a force in the sport, and promoted short-track races, then became general manager/promoter of the Charlotte Motor Speedway in 1975. He is an astute observer of the sport and why it appeals to so many people.

"Even though there's more competition for the dollar, stock car racing works today for the same reason it worked in the 1940s and the 1950s, and right on through the 1960s, 1970s, and 1980s. The lure of fast, colorful cars and fast, colorful drivers is a bond with fans that has not changed.

"What we have to be careful about is to keep the sawdust in it. We don't want to make it an antiseptic deal like Formula 1 has become. People like to see other people doing dangerous things, that's all there is to it. We have to work hard to keep the color in it."

The View from Dover Downs

Al Robinson is the marketing and public relations manager at Dover Downs International Speedway in Delaware. He has a seldom-seen passion for the sport. A passion so deep it takes him coast to coast and border to border just to watch a race. But unlike most NASCAR-watchers, his passion extends to competition on the hundreds of obscure dirt tracks that dot the countryside. He's seen as many races as almost anyone, and he's a font of motorsports information and opinions.

"Stock car racing has worked since its inception, but the scale increased incrementally in the 1970s and dramatically in the 1980s. And it works because it provides fans with a quality product that's something like a morality play.

"The vast majority of fans have a favorite something: a favorite driver or a favorite brand of car. Driver fans outnumber car fans, but there are still people who'd rather push a Ford than drive a Chevy and vice versa. That's why every one of those laps is an installment in the struggle between good and evil. If you're an Earnhardt fan and he goes a lap down, every lap is part of his struggle for him to regain his rightful place at the head of the field. It's tragedy if he crashes and goes to the garage, but it's still drama.

"It's theater on a grander scale than most other professional sports, and it also provides for a multitude of rooting interests. When there are two football or baseball teams playing, there are only two rooting interests. In a race, you have rooting interest for drivers, for cars, and, to some extent, for sponsors. And if your favorite drops out, you can always go to your second-favorite and keep rooting right to the end. If a baseball or football game gets out of hand, who are you going to cheer for the rest of the day?

"To this point, racing has remained financially accessible and loyal to a blue-collar audience. That may be changing, but it's been a sport for the people up to this point. I think that's one of the keys to its popularity, being a sport for the people. Fans look at drivers and crewmen and owners as less snobbish or egotistical or greedy than stick-and-ball players. Richard Petty started that by standing as a role model—the dominant role model, in fact—and a very good one for those who followed.

"There have been some drivers perceived as less-than-perfect role models, but their flaws were usually flaws of ordinary people. The only example of someone who fell from grace and brought disrepute upon racing was Tim Richmond. To some people, though, he's still seen as a tragic figure rather than one who brought the sport into disrepute.

"To put it another way: We complain about drivers who whine or say nasty words on television. Those things are lesser character faults than being wife-beaters and drug dealers. Because of that, it's become easier to sell racing to sponsors. There was a time when sponsorship was limited to automotive-related corporations or those with demographics that paralleled race fans.

"The first great revolution was from R.J. Reynolds, not only for its expenditure and loyalty, but because it was one of the first prominent non-automotive sponsors. The second revolution was led by Procter and Gamble with its Tide sponsorship of Darrell Waltrip. The arrival of consumer products as sponsors was in recognition and anticipation of the number of women becoming race fans. Only a couple of the 40 to 45 Winston Cup sponsors aren't marketing directly to the public. If you place them beside the roster of IndyCar sponsors, you'll see that NASCAR's sponsors are consumer product manufacturers selling to the American marketplace.

"There's been a snowball effect. The success of automotive products led in the 1970 and early 1980s to the marketing of non-automotive and male-oriented products. By the late 1980s, there was marketing of products that not only weren't automotive, but not even male oriented. We've really gone mainstream, and there seems to be a limitless tolerance for corporate sponsorship.

"That's good for a lot of reasons, but there's danger in the headlong rush to absorb all that corporate money. We have to be sure that the soul of the sport—what those 42 cars do out there every weekend—isn't lost or obscured by the clutter."

Stock car legends live and breathe in NASCAR, doing much more than attending jersey retirement parties or participating in the occasional ceremonial parade onto the playing field. Richard Petty, shown here with son Kyle in 1979, can be found at the track pretty much any weekend of the year, overseeing his race team. The same can be said for dozens of legendary figures who went from driving cars to owning a team.

According to industry insider Tom Cotter, NASCAR racing's near-weekly races and constant drama attract fans much like a soap opera draws viewers. "There are 42 different stories every weekend, and the fans can't wait to see what happens in the next episode," Cotter said.

PREVIOUS: Bill Elliott won the 1985 Daytona 500, the first leg in what later became his successful quest for the inaugural Winston Million bonus.

Kyle Petty (on the right, with Richard and Lee Petty), is the third generation of the Pettys to have a successful NASCAR career. His son, 17-year-old Adam, is carrying on the family name.

After 17 years of trying, Darrell Waltrip finally won his coveted Daytona 500 in 1988. His fuel strategy worked to perfection, which led to his version of the "Icky Shuffle" in victory lane.

500 at Talladega, and the Mountain Dew Southern 500 at Darlington. (Along with the Coca-Cola World 600 at the Charlotte Motor Speedway, they made up the four legs of the Winston Million.)

Elliott's dramatic victory at Darlington on Labor Day weekend of 1985 gave NASCAR one of its most spectacular moments. Not only did he win the Mountain Dew Southern 500 at the sport's toughest track, it came on national television and before a huge media contingent. The story was so compelling—and the timing perfect since not much else was going on that weekend—that *Sports Illustrated* put Elliott on its cover, the first time it had put a stock car driver out front. Alas, the SI jinx held: Despite winning the Winston Million and 11 races, Elliott lost the series championship to Waltrip at the season-ending race in California.

The 1980s were years of transition. Seven-time champion and 200-race-winner Richard Petty won his last race, in July 1984 at Daytona Beach. Three-time champion and winner of 83 races, Cale Yarborough retired after the 1988 season to become a car owner. David Pearson, a three-time champion and winner of 105 races, finally retired after the 1986 season. Although he would drive several more races, Donnie Allison's career as a contender effectively ended in a

Wisconsin native Dick Trickle has been a full-schedule Winston Cup driver since 1989. After years of success on the ASA circuit, Trickle was summoned to the South to replace the injured Mike Alexander on the Stavola brothers-owned team. Ironically, Alexander was filling in for Bobby Allison, who had been critically injured in the summer of 1988 at Pocono, Pennsylvania. Trickle has driven for a handful of owners, most recently the Virginia-based Ford team of Junie Donlavey.

Teammates but hardly the best of friends on the Junior Johnson-owned, Budweiser-sponsored team, Neil Bonnett (12) and Darrell Waltrip (11) raced each other hard every weekend. They were together—well, sort of—on Johnson's team during the 1984, 1985, and 1986 seasons. During that period Waltrip won 13 races and Bonnett 3. By 1987, they were gone, Waltrip to Hendrick Motorsports and Bonnett to Rahmoc.

Rusty Wallace (left) and Neil Bonnett before a race in the late 1980s. Bonnett was the fourth member of the fabled "Alabama Gang" that featured Bobby and Donnie Allison and Red Farmer. Never a big winner—20 poles and 18 races—Bonnett was nevertheless one of NASCAR's most popular and respected drivers. He won his share of major events—3 each near Atlanta and Rockingham, 2 each near Charlotte, Dover, and Richmond, and 1 each at Daytona Beach, Darlington, Talladega, Ontario, Pocono, and North Wilkesboro— but never challenged for the Winston Cup. A series of injuries slowed him in the late 1980s, and he died in a single-car accident while practicing for the 1994 Daytona 500.

financial ruin in 1983. But his career was revived when Jack Roush hired him in 1988, and Martin got his breakthrough victory late in 1989 at Rockingham. Kyle Petty emerged as an on-track star and the sport's most colorful individual even as Earnhardt began building his reputation as an unrelenting and unforgiving driver.

Most of the rookie of the year award winners in the 1980s turned out pretty well, among them: Geoff Bodine, Sterling Marlin, Rusty Wallace, Ken Schrader, and Dick Trickle. Short-track stars Jody Ridley and Ron Bouchard each won once before fading from the Winston Cup scene in the late 1980s, and Ken Bouchard also had a short

violent crash at Charlotte in May 1981— ironically, in a race his brother, Bobby, won. Indy car driver Tim Richmond burst into stock car racing in 1981, won 13 races in the next six years, then was banned because NASCAR suspected he had AIDS. He died in 1989, reportedly of complications from the disease, which had been diagnosed in 1987.

Former national champion Benny Parsons got his 21st and last victory in 1984, the year after Bill Elliott got the first of his 40. Harry Gant, who would become one of the tour's most popular drivers, got the first of his 18 career victories in 1982. It was a bad-news/good-news decade for Mark Martin. He failed with his own team and approached

and not-so-sweet career. But tragedy struck twice, taking 1986 Rookie of the Year Alan Kulwicki and 1987 Rookie of the Year Davey Allison in separate air crashes in 1993.

Some have compared the growth and maturing of Winston Cup racing to a drive from Boston to Daytona Beach. Using that analysis, it's clear the 1940s took the sport just down the road, perhaps to Providence, Rhode Island. The 1950s advanced it into New York City, the 1960s got it to Washington, D.C., and the 1970s delivered it into the Carolinas. Few would deny that the 1980s took NASCAR racing deep into Florida, leaving precious little more of the trip for the 1990s.

Bobby Allison has seen stock car racing from the top as well as the bottom. His 85 Winston Cup/Grand National victories put him third on the list behind Petty and David Pearson, and Allison has been a player in some of the most significant races in NASCAR history. He also has been a magnet for tragedy, losing sons Davey and Clifford and experiencing several horrific accidents. Allison waited a long time for his first championship, with five second-place season finishes to his credit before winning the Winston Cup championship in 1983.

Tim Richmond was fast, flamboyant, and a fan favorite during his brief time in NASCAR. He won 14 poles and 13 races for owners Raymond Beadle and Rick Hendrick between 1983 and his final season of 1987.

By the mid-1980s, Dale Earnhardt evolved from a young phenom to a living legend. Here, the seven-time NASCAR champion talks things over with three-time championship owner Rick Hendrick in 1985 at the Charlotte Motor Speedway.

Tim Richmond enjoyed his first taste of NASCAR success with team owner Raymond Beadle and backing from Pontiac and Old Milwaukee.

One of the best teams in all of
stock car racing is that of Dale
Earnhardt and team owner
Richard Childress. Here, the
Childress crew gives Earnhardt pit
service at North Wilkesboro in the
spring of 1985.

MYTHS

Although all sports are subject to the usual misinformed banter, NASCAR seems to be rife with more misconceptions than most. Hopefully, this section will help to amend some of these often-believed but far-from-true perceptions.

MYTH #1

Race Drivers Are Not Athletes

Years ago, at the height of his career—and when he was younger and more fit—Richard Petty was asked if he was an athlete. After all, the skeptic pointed out, race drivers simply sit down and steer. The car and its engine do all the hard work. The questioner had looked around the nearby garage area and noticed a bunch of 30- to 50-year-old men who didn't appear to have an athletic gene among 'em.

Petty had heard the question before, so his answer was ready. He described in great detail the strength and cardiovascular conditioning required to race upwards of 600 miles in the middle of the summer. He explained about upper-body strength and eye-hand coordination, and spoke eloquently about reaction time, stamina, and the determination to excel. When the man still didn't seem convinced, Petty issued a challenge.

"Well, try this," he said. "Put on a woolen sweatsuit, shoes, gloves, and a helmet, then get in your family car at noon one day in the middle of July. Roll up all the windows except the left-front, turn the heater wide open, and crank the radio as loud as it'll go. Then drive around in rush-hour traffic for four hours without stopping except for 20 seconds every half hour for gas and tires. And try not to hit anybody or get hit while you're at it."

Petty's point was well taken. Not only must race drivers have great strength and stamina to withstand searing heat and humidity, they must have enormous powers of concentration. If driving 500 miles at 180 miles per hour in the midst of 40 other impatient drivers isn't athletic, then what is? If race drivers aren't athletes, then surely golfers and bowlers aren't either. Skillful, to be sure; but athletic? Not a chance.

Kyle Petty was an outstanding high school football and basketball player, good enough to receive some NCAA Division I scholarship

Stock car racing has long been viewed as a southern-born and -bred sport despite being a nation-wide phenomenon for quite some time. Fred Lorenzen, one of NASCAR's early stars, was from Elmhurst, Illinois, a Chicago suburb.

offers. Is he any less an athlete now than when he was a stick-and-ball star? "This can be every bit as demanding as football or basketball," he says of stock car racing. "It might be a different kind of physical demand, but there's a severe demand just the same. Run 500 miles at Dover in June, then drag your butt out of that race car and tell me that what you've just done wasn't athletic."

Two-time Daytona 500 winner Dale Jarrett was such a good amateur golfer that he toyed with the idea of turning pro. Given a few days to polish his game, he could play 18 holes with anybody on the PGA Tour and not embarrass himself. Even with some coaching, it's unlikely Tiger Woods or Greg Norman or Fred Couples could get in Jarrett's race car and even remotely approach the speeds he runs every weekend.

And so it goes, on and on.

Gadsden, Alabama, native Steve Grissom was good enough in high school to attract the attention of football coaches at Alabama and Auburn. Likewise, Bobby Hillin was a standout linebacker in Midland, Texas, considered one of the best high school football areas in America. Sterling Marlin played football in Columbia, Tennessee; Geoff Bodine played in Waverly, New York; and Ernie Irvan played football and tennis during his high school years in Modesto, California. Except for a knee injury, 1990 Daytona 500 winner Derrike Cope might have been a major league catcher. Joe Nemechek played four sports in high school and looks like he could pick up right where he left off.

Race drivers generally score above average on tests for reaction time, situational recognition, and peripheral awareness. Generally, their hand-eye coordination and ability to recognize and respond to unusual situations are better developed than most "mainstream" athletes.

MYTH #2
Only Southerners Know How to Race

This is sort of like saying that only Canadians know how to play hockey or Brazilians know how to play soccer. In truth, many of stock car racing's best and most popular drivers began their career well outside the Southeast, the acknowledged heartland of the sport.

The long-retired Fred Lorenzen, for example, was from Elmhurst, a suburb of Chicago. Former Daytona 500 winner Pete Hamilton was from Massachusetts, which also sent brothers Ken and Ron Bouchard to Southern stock car racing in the 1980s. Ricky Craven is from Maine, Jimmy Spencer and John Andretti from Pennsylvania, and the late Rob Moroso and Grand National star Randy LaJoie are from Connecticut.

The three Bodine brothers learned to race in upstate New York, and the three Wallace brothers and long-time friend Ken Schrader competed in the area around St. Louis. The two Labonte brothers and Bobby Hillin are from Texas, as was oft-time NASCAR winner A.J. Foyt. The Upper Midwest has produced several drivers: Dave Marcis, Dick Trickle, Ted Musgrave, and the late Alan Kulwicki are from Wisconsin, and former Rookie of the Year Johnny Benson is from Michigan. The long-retired Hutchison brothers—Ron and Dick—are from Keokuk, Iowa, also home to former journeyman driver Ramo Stott. The late Tiny Lund, a former Daytona 500 winner, was from Harlan, Iowa.

Derrike Cope and Chad Little began their racing careers in Washington. IndyCar and stock car racer Wally Dallenbach is from Colorado,

Ernie Irvan, Jeff Gordon, and Robby Gordon (not related) are from California, and Mark Martin is from Arkansas. Three of the last five Winston Cup champions before 1997 were born and reared away from the Southeast: Terry Labonte in 1996, Jeff Gordon in 1995, and Kulwicki in 1992.

MYTH #3
Stock Cars Are Just Like Street Cars

This is true if your street car is handmade to exacting standards and specifications, costs upward of $75,000, doesn't have many creature comforts, and gets terrible gas mileage. Truth be told, the only thing "stock" about a stock car is some of its sheet metal—and even that is bent and shaped to fit more snugly than Detroit ever intended. The hood, fenders, quarter panels, and grille are fairly close to stock, but that's about it.

Just how "unstock" are stock cars?

1. Most of today's street cars from Detroit have fuel-injected, V-6 engines and are front-wheel drive. In contrast, NASCAR cars use V-8 engines with carburetors, and run with rear-wheel-drive transmissions.

Richard Petty, trying to explain that stock car racing required ample stamina, once said, "Put on a woolen sweat suit, shoes, gloves, and a helmet, then get in your family car at noon one day in the middle of July. Roll up all the windows except the left-front, turn the heater wide open, and crank the radio as loud as it'll go. Then drive around in rush-hour traffic for 4 hours without stopping except for 20 seconds every half hour for gas and tires. And try not to hit anybody or get hit while you're at it."

MYTHS

2. NASCAR cars are longer, wider, lower, and lighter than their street-legal cousins. While the silhouettes of race cars vaguely resemble those of street cars, they aren't likely to be identical at any two points. (When's the last time you saw a 6-inch aluminum spoiler across the back of a Pontiac Grand Prix?).

3. NASCAR cars are single-seaters with only a handful of gauges. There's a tachometer, water, oil-pressure and temperature gauges, fuel-pressure gauge, and rpm limiter. There's no radio (other than the two-way radio between the driver and his crew), heater, air conditioner (they wish), windshield wipers, headlights, brake lights, or air bags.

4. Assembly lines being what they are, Detroit can crank out a street car in less than an hour. From start to finish, you can't get a race-ready NASCAR car in less than two weeks, even if your order goes to the head of the line.

MYTH #4

Stock Car Racing Is a Regional Sport

True, but only if the region in question stretches from Canada to Mexico, from the Atlantic Ocean to Japan, and just about everywhere else. The fact that stock car races attract huge crowds at every venue—but not as many as local law-enforcement agencies often estimate—proves its appeal is far from regional.

Try telling people in Maine, New Hampshire, and the rest of New England that stock car racing is a regional sport. Better yet, look at the number of license plates from New England at tracks in the Southeast and Midwest. Not only do New Englanders flock to superspeedways at Loudon, New Hampshire, and Watkins Glen, New York, they think nothing of driving to Virginia and the Carolinas to watch races.

If stock car racing is a Southeastern thing, how do you explain 275,000 fans at the Brickyard 400 at Indianapolis or the almost 100,000 at the Michigan International Speedway twice a year? Or the 185,000 at Texas Motor Speedway, the near-sellouts at Sears Point and Fontana on the West Coast, and Phoenix in the Southwest. If racing is primarily a Southern phenomenon,

what's with the twice-a-year throngs for Winston Cup races in Delaware and Pennsylvania?

Granted, the first 3 races in NASCAR's inaugural season of 1949 were contested in the Southeast. But that 8-race season also included two events in Pennsylvania and another in New York. Of the 19 races run the next year, 9 were in the Southeast and 10 in the Northeast and Midwest. Of the 41 races run in 1951, more were run in the Northeast, Midwest, and on the West Coast than in the Southeast.

The current schedule is tilted more to the Southeast, but only slightly. Of the 32 races on the 1997 Winston Cup schedule, 18 were scheduled at tracks in Florida, Georgia, Alabama, the Carolinas, Tennessee and Virginia. The other 14 were in Delaware, Pennsylvania, New York, New Hampshire, Michigan, Indiana, California, Arizona, and Texas.

It seems only a matter of time before the schedule either grows to perhaps 35 races a year, or some of the current venues will lose dates. A spanking-new superspeedway in Las Vegas begs for a Winston Cup date. Likewise, the new superspeedway across the Mississippi River from St. Louis—home to long-time NASCAR player Anheuser-Busch—seems a natural for a Winston Cup date. And the Homestead Motorsports Complex just south of Miami would deliver big-time stock car racing into yet another new market.

MYTH #5

Bootlegging Led Directly to Stock Car Racing

This makes about as much sense as saying muggings led to professional boxing. Granted, some bootleggers occasionally raced in the sport's early years, but they represented only a fraction of the men (and women) who populated the sport in its early days. The long-held misconception that most of stock car racing's pioneers made or hauled illegal liquor was fueled by the oft-told stories about Hall of Fame driver/owner Junior Johnson. A native of Wilkes County, North Carolina, he served time in a federal penitentiary in Ohio for making and hauling moonshine. Because of that, some students of the sport's early years jumped to the conclusion that bootlegging and racing went hand-in-hand.

That's not to say the sport didn't have its share of rouges and scoundrels. And some of them openly lived on the other side of the law, more concerned with making a living than whether it was legal. In the post-Prohibition and pre-World War II South, the manufacture and distribution of non-tax-paid liquor was considered a victimless crime. Many counties in the Deep South were dry, even after Prohibition was lifted in 1933. But the difficulty of getting "government" liquor in the big cities and the ever-growing clamor for moonshine inspired bootleggers to take greater risks transporting the brew from their mountain stills to distributors in cities like Atlanta, Asheville, Greensboro, Charlotte, Nashville, Columbia, and Roanoke.

Like Johnson, Lloyd Seay was another bootlegger who made a name for himself during a brief but glorious racing career. Just 18 and a native of Dawsonville, Georgia, he rose to stardom in the early 1940s with victories on dirt tracks in Deland, Florida; Allentown, Pennsylvania; Greensboro and High Point, North Carolina. He was seventh, fourth, and first in 1941 races on the Daytona Beach highway/beach course, then won at High Point and Lakewood Speedway in Atlanta over Labor Day weekend of that year. But he came to an untimely end when a 29-year-old cousin murdered him after arguing about an unpaid bill for moonshine ingredients.

Fellow Georgians Roy Hall and Bob and Tim Flock also raced and hauled liquor from time to time in the 1940s. In later years, Virginians Wendell Scott and Buddy Arrington went from hauling to racing—and back and forth. Clay Earles and Enoch Staley did some hauling in the rough and tumble years before they built and managed successful speedways. So while a handful of drivers and promoters might have made or hauled moonshine, the relationship between moonshine and stock car racing wasn't nearly as close as Hollywood and Southern folklore would have us believe.

"It's been overplayed to some extent," says Humpy Wheeler of the Charlotte Motor Speedway, "but it was still something of a factor. Bootleggers primarily used Fords, most of them built from '33 or '34 into the 1940s, when the war broke out. Those cars were adaptable to bigger engines and hydraulic brakes and modified transmissions, things the bootlegger needed to outrun the cops. As bootlegging began to fade away, those people were drawn to stock car racing."

So the relationship, then, was more technical than anything else. Bootleggers were an innovative lot, hands-on mechanics who relied heavily on their cars to keep them one step ahead of the law. They couldn't afford to have an engine quit, or brakes fail, or a radiator overheat during a late-night dash from their hidden still to their customers.

The car that won the very first 'Strictly Stock' race was disqualified by NASCAR inspectors because its rear springs were spread. "Spring spreading" was an old bootleggers' trick to keep the back of their car at acceptable street height while fully loaded. It also helped stabilize the car during high-speed runs through treacherous mountain roads.

Yup, this shot of Robert Mitchum on the set of *Thunder Road* is the popular image of the origins of stock car racing. Bootleggers learned how to drive fast outrunning the law, and they turned their talents into race driving careers, right? Not quite. A few early stars were most definitely in that line of work, but stock car racing came to be because some folks liked to go fast, and a bunch of others liked to watch.

Geoff Bodine graduated from
NASCAR's northeastern-based
Modified tour to become a
Winston Cup star. His biggest
triumph was in the 1986 Daytona
500 for team owner Rick
Hendrick.

Kyle Petty was the first third-generation NASCAR driver to succeed in the sport his grandfather, Lee, and father, Richard, helped build. Kyle won the very first race he ever ran, an ARCA 200 at Daytona Beach in 1979. His family brought him along slowly, limiting his Winston Cup involvement until finally approving a full-schedule effort for the first time in 1981. He drove for Petty Enterprises, the Wood Brothers, and Team Sabco before creating his own team—PE2—for the 1997 season. He won twice for the Wood Brothers and seven times for Sabco. Among his hobbies: leading several hundred motorcyclists across country each spring to raise money for children's charities.

Kyle Petty drove the Wood Brothers' No. 21 car from 1985 to 1988, winning two races in four years. Petty signing with the Wood Brothers wasn't quite the equivalent of a Hatfield marrying a McCoy, but it was close. The Petty and Wood families rubbed fenders in NASCAR competition for several generations, beginning with drivers Lee Petty and Glen Wood racing in the 1950s. Richard Petty carried the tradition on by vying for titles against Wood Brothers' cars in the 1960s, and Petty Enterprises and the Wood Brothers continue the rivalry in Winston Cup competition through to today.

By the late 1980s, Winston Cup cars bore the sleek lines of today's cars, as well as the logos of mainstream sponsors. The influx of corporate money pushed small-time backers out of the picture and brought lap times down and qualifying speeds up. Then, just as now, you had to pay to play with the big boys.

RIGHT: Cale Yarborough won 4 Daytona 500s for 3 different owners but was 10th in the 1987 race in his own car. He enjoyed great success with the Wood Brothers in the late 1960s but left them to try his hand at Indy car racing. He joined Junior Johnson for a sensational 8-year, 3-championship, 55-victory run (1973–1980) before deciding to trim back his racing and spend more time with his wife and school-age daughters. He drove a few years for M. C. Anderson, then retired altogether after the 1988 season to form his own team.

Ken Schrader has a well-earned reputation for wanting to race as often as possible. A former Midwestern short-track star, this St. Louis native first went NASCAR racing in 1985—his Rookie of the Year season—with veteran owner Junie Donlavey. In 1988, after proving himself with Donlavey's underfinanced team, Schrader accepted a call to join the potent Hendrick Motorsports empire. All four of his Cup victories have come in Hendrick-prepared cars. There's nothing to indicate Schrader was any better with Hendrick than with Donlavey—or Andy Petree, who he would later become associated with. But Hendrick's well-heeled team wanted for nothing and gave Schrader what he needed to get to victory lane.

Terry Labonte wins at North
Wilkesboro in 1988. Few
champions in any motorsports
discipline have carried the "nice
guys finish first" label with more
grace and dignity than Labonte.
A native of Corpus Christi, Texas,
he came to North Carolina in
1978 to drive for Louisiana oil
speculator Billy Hagan. All he did
was finish fourth in his NASCAR
debut at the Southern 500, then
come in seventh and ninth in his
next two starts that fall. He and
Hagan won the 1984 Winston
Cup, but when the team's future
grew uncertain, Labonte left to
spend three years with Junior
Johnson. A year with the Richard
Jackson team and a brief return
to Hagan preceded Labonte's
move to Hendrick Motorsports,
where he won the 1996
championship. He remains one of
NASCAR's most low-key and
gracious drivers, but also one of
its most competitive.

Bobby Allison was driving the Stavola brothers-owned No. 22 Miller-sponsored Buick when his career ended after a vicious crash at Pocono, Pennsylvania, in the summer of 1988.

Cale Yarborough was the only driver to win three consecutive Winston Cups, doing it with owner Junior Johnson in 1976, 1977, and 1978. He also won 70 poles and 83 races.

Mark Martin returned to NASCAR in 1987 with owner Jack Roush and immediately stamped himself a star of the future. His first foray into Winston Cup had been in 1981 and 1982 with his own team.

Rusty Wallace got a controversial victory in the 1989 Winston All-Star race at the Charlotte Motor Speedway. He bumped past leader Darrell Waltrip in the final laps for his only victory in the annual event.

CHAPTER SIX

Mark Martin has developed into one of the
Winston Cup tour's most capable drivers on
tracks of all types and distances. As the sport
moved into the 1990s, it left its short-track roots
even further behind in favor of larger venues in
more sponsor-friendly markets. Drivers like Martin
were forced to adapt to everything from road
courses to banked superspeedways, from
relatively flat superspeedways to high-banked
ovals. A former short-track champion from
Arkansas, Martin entered 1998 having done
virtually everything in NASCAR racing except win
a Winston Cup. It is, almost everyone agrees,
only a matter of time.

THE 19 90s

The Golden Age of Stock Car Racing

It's hard to pinpoint the exact moment the first NASCAR fan said, "I'll bet (fill in the name of almost any driver here) is already home by now. And here we are, still stuck in the same traffic jam we were stuck in two hours ago." Or when the first fan said, "You know, it's almost impossible to get close to (fill in the name of almost any driver here) nowadays. And by the way, who are all those people surrounding him?"

As the 1980s turned into the 1990s, those people surrounding the driver were most likely his booking agent, business manager, investment advisor, team public relations/media coordinator, office secretary, pilot, and personal trainer.

ABOVE: Mark Martin enjoys the thrill of yet another victory lane celebration in the fall of 1992 at the Charlotte Motor Speedway. By the opening of the 1998 season, Martin had won 35 Winston Cup poles and 22 races, all but two of the poles and all 22 of the victories with team owner Jack Roush. He's so good in the Busch Series that he is the division's all-time winningest driver despite running barely a third of the events on Saturdays before Cup races at the same venue.

The start of the spring 1990 short-track race at North Wilkesboro Speedway. Mark Martin and Geoff Bodine started 1-2, but 20th-starting Brett Bodine won the 400-lapper.

Somewhere in that mass of humanity was a wife (or significant other) and maybe a child wondering why Daddy always had to bring along all these people everywhere he went.

That's a good question.

It was sometime between the late 1980s and the early 1990s that stock car racing—once the most unfettered and unsophisticated form of all motorsports—went big time. The sport (or was it more a business by then?) became such a massive marketing tool throughout the 1980s that drivers were forced to surround themselves with administrative help. Their sponsor wanted them one place, their car manufacturer wanted them somewhere else, the series sponsor needed them over here for just a moment, and the race sponsor wanted them over there for a few minutes.

No longer do drivers work on their own cars during the week, help the crew chief drive the hauler to the track, then help set up the car for qualifying and the race. You also won't see drivers hanging around after a race to sign autographs for fans and pose for pictures. These are all part of the past. The drivers' post-race schedule now goes something like this: sprint from their race car to the team hauler to change clothes, utter a few words of wisdom for a team PR representative to pass on to the media, grab a briefcase, jump into a waiting car, and dash to the nearest airport where a personal jet is warmed up and ready to go.

Before the last team's hauler is loaded and inching its way through traffic, the driver is already back home. After all, he has to rest up for a grueling week of personal appearances, autograph sessions, TV talk show interviews, and the photo shoot for his latest endorsement. All of which he is paid to do. And, by the way, there's another race next weekend. Better get your sleep. Those two hours in the Lear jet can be tough.

NASCAR GOES INTO ORBIT

Big-time stock car racing moved from the 1980s into the 1990s as effortlessly as a sharp knife moves through hot butter. No fuss, no muss, and hardly a whimper of complaint

from anyone. Indeed, NASCAR seemed to be living a charmed life. It entered the 1990s more popular and prosperous than ever, all the while seemingly free of the economic problems and public relations scandals so common in other sports. In many ways, it might considered the sport's Golden Age.

There's no denying that by the early 1990s Americans had embraced Winston Cup racing to a degree unimaginable in any other form of racing. *Sports Illustrated* even climbed down from its Eastern Establishment pedestal long enough to boldly

proclaim NASCAR as the fastest-growing sport in America. And while that may be stretching it a bit, the very fact that SI would make that statement and begin paying more attention to NASCAR spoke volumes.

The groundwork for the sport's impressive growth was laid in the 1980s, when a handful of Fortune 500 companies dropped by to see what it was all about. Their marketing people found the landscape so hospitable, and the prospects for long-term growth so bright, they decided it might be worth a gamble or two. One success story

led to another, and before long many of the country's biggest and brightest companies had found NASCAR a good way to market everything from antacid to hamburgers, from beer to health care.

By the midpoint of the 1990s, almost all of Winston Cup's 45 or so full-schedule teams had at least one solid, well-heeled, national-level sponsor. The old standbys— some from as far back as the 1970s, but most of them from the 1980s—remained a fixture: Anheuser-Busch, Procter and Gamble, Skoal, Valvoline, Miller Brewing,

Dale Earnhardt rolled into the 1990s as NASCAR's big gun. Firing on both barrels in 1991, Earnhardt banged home the Winston Cup after winning it by almost 200 points over Ricky Rudd. All told, Earnhardt has seven Cups, six of them with team owner Richard Childress, the other with Rod Osterlund.

OPPOSITE TOP: Each year's two Winston Cup races at the Talladega Superspeedway are traditionally among the closest, most competitive, and most controversial of any races during the season. The 2.66-mile track east of Birmingham has been the scene of incredible photo-finish shootouts, a handful of unexpected winners (James Hylton, Lennie Pond, Dick Brooks, Ron Bouchard, Phil Parsons, Bobby Hillin, and Richard Brickhouse) and some of the most spectacular and frightening crashes in modern-day stock car racing. Some say the high-banked, super-fast track was doomed in 1968 when ground was broken atop what local legend said was a sacred Indian burial ground. When the track's 1969 opener was hit by the only boycott in NASCAR history, local historians merely winked and smiled knowingly.

Coors, STP, Kodiak, Citgo, Kodak, GMC/Goodwrench, and Texaco Havoline.

Joining them in the 1990s were such heavyweights as DuPont, Kellogg's, Pennzoil, Circuit City, Western Auto, Exide, MBNA, McDonald's, RCA, Maxwell House, Ford Motor Co., Hooters, and Raybestos. Granted, some companies were disappointed by the return on their investment and didn't stay long. But by 1998, most of the sponsors who had come aboard early in the decade seemed committed for the long haul. This was good news, given the ever-increasing cost of fielding teams.

THE MEDIA BLITZ

Credit for some of the economic windfall must go to increased attention from radio, television, and the print media. Between 1979 and 1990, NASCAR went from being on live television only a few times annually to having cable and major networks fighting for rights to televise every race. After this development, fans in every far-flung American outpost could see every points race—live in its entirety—plus special events like the Busch Clash and The Winston. Almost every cable network also developed its own NASCAR-related "news magazine" to further publicize the sport and its sponsors.

Several radio networks expanded their coverage to include every points race and special event, as well as pole day qualifying updates and daily reports on the latest goings-on within the sport. Additionally, the daily newspapers in America's biggest cities (among them: New York, Los Angeles, Miami, Dallas-Fort Worth, Tampa, Boston, Kansas City, and Cleveland) began paying closer attention to stock car racing. Not to be outdone by the dailies, a handful of monthly magazines and tabloids relating to NASCAR began publishing.

In most cases, the sport has responded well to the pressure and public scrutiny brought on by its popularity. Unlike most stick-and-ball sports, NASCAR has maintained an almost squeaky clean image. Publicly it is virtually drug free, almost completely untainted by domestic battery or spousal abuse charges, and relatively free of even the most minor traffic problems. The most notable recent exception is team

Ex-NFL coach Joe Gibbs has enjoyed great success with his No. 18 Chevrolet team, first with Dale Jarrett and most recently with Bobby Labonte. He also owns highly successful NHRA Top Fuel and Funny Car drag racing teams.

With competition at an all-time high, quick and accurate pit stops play a vital role in the success of a Winston Cup team. There was a time when pit stops were an afterthought, a necessary interruption to racing. But as on-track competition grew more intense in the 1970s, savvy crew chiefs realized that every second saved in the pits was worth several hundred yards on the race track. The Wood brothers elevated pit stops to an art form, often changing tires and refueling their cars without losing a lap. Today, teams often have a handful of crew members whose only job is to pit the car on race days. They may have some shop responsibilities, but their number one job is to change four tires, dump in 22 gallons of fuel, and get their driver back on the track as quick as humanly possible.

Davey Allison won 14 poles and 19 races in only 191 starts and most certainly was going to be a NASCAR star deep into the next millennium. But he was killed when his helicopter crashed trying to land at the Talladega Superspeedway in July 1993. After running a few Winston Cup races in 1985 and 1986 and then most of the 1987 schedule (winning at Talladega and Dover), he joined the tour full-time in 1988. He spent the rest of his career with Robert Yates, and what a formidable combination they became, winning on short tracks, high-banked superspeedways, relatively flat superspeedways, and mid-length, moderately-banked superspeedways.

Alan Kulwicki died in an airplane crash in Tennessee just four months after being honored as NASCAR's 1992 champion. One of Winston Cup's best-educated and most analytical drivers, the Wisconsin native and former national short-track champion, brought all his worldly belongings south to go racing in 1985. He chose to do it his way, building and running his own team instead of driving for others who might not see things exactly his way. Times were tough for a while, but Kulwicki exalted when he got his breakthrough victory at Phoenix in the fall of 1988. He won once in 1990 and 1991, then twice in his championship season of 1992. He won the title by 10 points, the closest finish in series history, and he did it by leading the most laps and finishing second to points runner-up Bill Elliott in the 1992 finale near Atlanta.

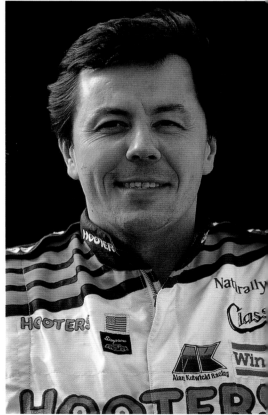

owner Rick Hendrick, whose financial problems with the federal government were well documented. After emphatically declaring his innocence of a myriad of charges, the Charlotte businessman plead guilty in August 1997. On the last day of the year, a federal district court judge sentenced him to a year of home detention, three years of probation, and a $250,000 fine.

Hendrick was accused of money laundering, mail fraud, bribery, and conspiracy involving his business dealings with Honda Motor Co. According to court documents, he offered bribes to corporate executives in exchange for preferential treatment when it came to the distribution of Honda's top-of-the-line models. While the case lingered in the courts for eight months, Hendrick Motorsports didn't miss a beat, winning the 1996 Winston Cup with Terry Labonte and the 1997 title with teammate Jeff Gordon. (Hendrick was diagnosed with leukemia in November 1996 and hasn't been to a race since late that season.)

And unlike its stick-and-ball cousins, NASCAR has been relatively free of labor-management strife. There's been no work stoppage and only a few instances in which the sanctioning body had to fine or discipline any of its competitors. It's almost as if everyone realizes they're sitting on a golden egg, one they're wise enough to leave undisturbed. The series' only "strike" in the fall of 1969 at Talladega was such a dismal failure that the likelihood of another is almost zero.

That's not to say the sport doesn't have its problems. The drivers feel purses are inadequate, the February-through-Novem-

Richard Petty started second and led the opening laps of the 1992 Pepsi 400 in Daytona Beach, his final appearance at the famous 2.5-mile track where he won 10 races. Popular and revered almost beyond belief, Petty announced in 1991 that the 1992 season would be his last as a driver. His season-long "Fan Appreciation Tour" (some called it his "Income Appreciation Tour") saw the seven-time champion honored in almost every imaginable way at every stop on the tour. The merchandising arm and publicity arm of Petty Enterprises created hundreds of Fan Appreciation Tour items that fans gobbled up, each anxious to have something to commemorate the King's final ride.

ber schedule is cumbersome, and in-season rules changes are unfair to everyone. "Purses aren't good enough now, they've never been good enough, and they'll never be good enough," says three-time series champion Darrell Waltrip, the sport's most articulate owner/driver. "That's the nature of racing, and NASCAR should do something before they run a bunch of people out of business. If a track can't sell enough tickets to generate an acceptable purse and still make money for its owners, then it shouldn't get Winston Cup dates."

Equally troubling to some is the growing trend away from single-car teams. It's nothing new, witness the many years Petty Enterprises fielded two cars and the 1955 and 1956 seasons Carl Kiekhaefer fielded between two and six cars in every race. Both J.D. Stacy and Junior Johnson had multi-car teams in the 1980s, and Hendrick went from a single-car effort in 1984 to two full-schedule cars in 1986, then three cars beginning in 1987. Not to be outdone, Jack Roush went from one team in 1988 to two in 1992, three in 1996, and five for 1998. Felix Sabates' team grew from one car in 1989 to two for the 1993 and 1994 seasons, to three teams starting in 1997.

Suddenly, multi-car teams became all the rage. Robert Yates expanded to a two-car team in 1996 and Richard Childress added a

second team in 1997. Single-team owners Roger Penske and Michael Kranefuss merged their organizations for 1998, and Richard and Kyle Petty brought their separate teams under a family umbrella (although not under the same roof) in 1997. Even Bill Elliott, who hasn't enjoyed much success as a solo owner/driver, added a second team with rookie Jerry Nadeau (co-owned by NFL star Dan Marino) for the 1998 season.

Multi-car teams make economic sense. Corporate America loves winners, so owners who have enjoyed success with one team are generally approached first when new sponsors begin scouting business opportunities in NASCAR. The rich get richer while single-car owners like Ricky Rudd, Larry Morgan, Geoff Bodine, Larry Hedrick, Joe Gibbs, the Wood brothers, Bill Davis, Cale Yarborough, Chuck Rider, and Andy Petree move closer to NASCAR's endangered species list.

"If you find a sponsor willing to be part of a two- or three-car team, then go for it," says Davis, who fields Pontiacs for Ward Burton. "It doesn't cost twice as much to field a second car, especially if you already have the building, an administrative staff for your organization, and a crew. You've got to hire a few more people, but not another full crew. If the sponsor has enough money to spend, then you'd be foolish to not go for it. You don't exactly double your chances of making money, but it's close."

The other advantage involves technology, especially if crew chiefs, engine-builders, and drivers cooperate. With teams limited to seven test dates each year, organizations like Hendrick Motorsports (three teams), Roush Racing (five teams), or Sabco Racing (three teams) have an advantage over teams limited to seven dates. (NASCAR is looking closely at this, so don't be surprised if new rules limit an organization's number of tests.)

Roush, for example, can send Mark Martin and his crew to Talladega for a shock/spring test while Johnny Benson and his crew go to Martinsville for an engine test. When Martin and Benson are debriefed,

O. Bruton Smith posted a "speed limit" sign of 180 miles per hour when Richard Petty retired after the 1992 season-ending race at the Atlanta Motor Speedway. Smith is one of the sport's most visible track owners, never one to shy from the spotlight or a controversy. He helped build the Charlotte Motor Speedway in the early 1960s, left when it ran into financial problems, then returned in the early 1970s to make it the showplace of stock car racing. In recent years he's bought speedways in Georgia, California, and Tennessee, built (then almost rebuilt) the Texas Motor Speedway, and bought half-interest in a North Carolina short track which he and co-owner Bob Bahre closed.

Roush's other drivers, crew chiefs, and engine-builders sit in. Roush Racing thus gets chassis and engine data for five teams by using only two of its 35 allotted test dates.

After a decade in which no new speedways were built for Winston Cup, the 1990s saw tracks built in Loudon, New Hampshire; in the Dallas-Fort Worth area; Fontana, California; and Las Vegas, Nevada. In addition, tracks that have already hosted Busch or Craftsman races were built in Homestead, Florida; Fountain, Colorado; Orlando, Florida; and near Kansas City. By the mid-1990s, other tracks had been proposed near Atlantic City, New Jersey, and Baltimore, Maryland, and at two sites near Chicago.

The biggest venue news of the 1990s was the announcement in April 1993 of a long-rumored union of NASCAR and the venerable Indianapolis Motor Speedway. NASCAR president Bill France Jr. and IMS president Tony George finally agreed to run a 160-lap race (the Brickyard 400) on Saturday, August 6, 1994. It drew a

"POWER PEOPLE"

The cars and their drivers are the stars, but NASCAR would be nothing without a strong staff of on-site officials to make sure things get done right. Although there's not an ex-NASCAR driver among the lot of them, all have extensive background and experience in the inner workings of the sport.

Gary Nelson was a successful and innovative crew chief before becoming one of NASCAR's top officials. He has been Winston Cup director since the end of the 1993 season.

H. A. "Humpy" Wheeler, president of the Charlotte Motor Speedway is generally acknowledged as the most daring and innovative promoter in NASCAR. There is, almost literally, nothing he won't do to draw attention to his speedways and its three weekends of NASCAR racing each year.

Roger Penske has done it all: raced; owned successful sports car, Indy car, and stock car teams; owned and managed speedways; built speedways; and helped shape the face of motorsports in this country.

NASCAR president Bill France succeeded his father, "Big Bill" France, in January 1972. Stock car racing has enjoyed unprecedented growth in the years under his leadership.

Jack Roush, president of Roush Racing, oversees the preparation and race-day operations of five Winston Cup teams for Mark Martin, Ted Musgrave, Jeff Burton, Chad Little, and Johnny Benson.

Robert Yates began as a shop gofer and apprentice builder for the potent Holman-Moody team in the 1960s. He worked his way to team owner and has fielded cars for such recognized stars as Davey Allison, Dale Jarrett, Ernie Irvan, and 1998 Rookie of the Year candidate Kenny Irwin.

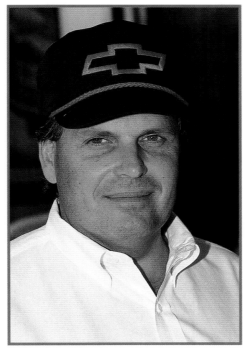

Although illness and legal problems may have weakened Rick Hendrick's grip on Hendrick Motorsports in recent years, his power and influence remain formidable. The multi-millionaire automobile dealer began creating his Chevrolet-based stock car empire in 1984 with Geoff Bodine. He's also fielded full-schedule teams for Tim Richmond, Darrell Waltrip, Benny Parsons, Ken Schrader, Ricky Rudd, Jeff Gordon, and Terry Labonte. He won the 1995 and 1997 Winston Cups with Jeff Gordon and the 1996 title with Labonte.

Driver-turned-owner Richard Childress has won six Winston Cup championships with driver Dale Earnhardt. His well-heeled RCR Inc. also fields a Winston Cup car for Mike Skinner and a Craftsman Series truck for Jay Sauter.

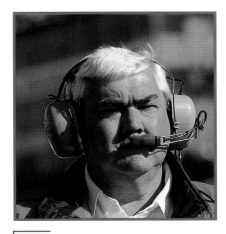

Junior Johnson went from being a convicted moonshiner to a successful driver to a championship team owner. His cars won three Winston Cups with Cale Yarborough at the wheel in the late 1970s and three with Darrell Waltrip in the early and mid-1980s.

Bill France surrounds himself with good people—then lets them do their jobs. One of his most trusted allies is Mike Helton, vice-president for competition.

Bruton Smith (left) and Humpy Wheeler are the brains, the ingenuity, and the power behind the unmatched growth of the Charlotte Motor Speedway over the past 20 years.

Gone, but not forgotten, Richard Petty was honorary starter for the 1993 Daytona 500, the first Winston Cup race since his retirement. Fittingly, his son, Kyle, started from the pole position.

The Roger Penske-owned team featuring Rusty Wallace switched from Pontiac to Ford sheet metal for the 1993 season. With manufacturers a necessary part of the sport—but not to the extent they were in the 1960s—teams feel more free to switch brands if one seems better than another. Wallace, for example, won most of his races in a Pontiac (the so-called red-headed stepchild of racing), but Penske felt Ford would be better in the long run.

NASCAR-record 300,000-plus fans and paid $5.4 million, by far the largest purse in Winston Cup history to that date. Hometown hero Jeff Gordon provided a fitting climax by winning, then celebrated by having pizza delivered to his room at the Speedway Motel.

It took one trip to Indy for the Brickyard 400 to become one of NASCAR's biggest events. Traditionally, drivers and owners have listed the Daytona 500 at Daytona Beach, the Coca-Cola World 600 at Charlotte, and the Mountain Dew Southern 500 at Darlington, as the races they most want to win. The Daytona 500 remains number one, but the choice among Indy, Charlotte, and Darlington for number two has become blurred. Thus far, only Gordon and Dale Earnhardt have won all four.

IN THE LIMELIGHT

At times it seemed nothing could stop NASCAR from stealing some of the attention once reserved for major league baseball and professional football, basketball, and hockey. Why, even such august publications as the *New York Times*, the *Washington Post*, the *Chicago Tribune*, and *USA Today* realized that stock car racing had progressed well beyond its backwoods, Southeastern roots. Weekly magazines like *Sports Illustrated*, *Time*, *Newsweek*, and *TV Guide* jumped on the bandwagon that had been forming since the Cale Yarbor-

Morgan Shepherd gave the famous Wood Brothers team a victory near Atlanta in the spring of 1993. It was the third of his four Cup victories, three of which have come at the 1.5-mile Atlanta Motor Speedway.

NEXT: Jeff Gordon and Ernie Irvan start 1-2 for the fall of 1993 race at the Charlotte Motor Speedway. Irvan went on to win in only his sixth start replacing the late Davey Allison at Robert Yates Racing.

and public relations themes built around the organization's 50th anniversary.

If a New York office wasn't enough to signal a change, then a series of exhibition races in Japan was. In 1995, after a series of meetings, officials of the Suzuka Circuit, the R.J. Reynolds Tobacco Co., and NASCAR agreed to run non-points, exhibition races in the fall of 1996, 1997, and 1998 at the road course in Suzuka. In addition, another non-points exhibition was scheduled for the fall of 1998 at the new oval track being built north of Tokyo. (Early in 1998, the likelihood of a third race at Suzuka faded. However, NASCAR stands firmly behind a November 1998 race at the oval at Motegi, Japan.)

Many teams don't embrace the idea of going to Japan with so many venues in the United States begging for dates. Bob Bahre's New Hampshire International Speedway (NHIS) at Loudon, New Hampshire, got its first Cup date in 1993 and a second race four years later. Bruton Smith's

The brightest moment in Michael Waltrip's career came when he won the Winston All-Star race at the Charlotte Motor Speedway in May 1996. It wasn't an official points victory, so Waltrip continues to be one of the losingest drivers in NASCAR history. He came into the 1998 season 0 for 362 and seldom in his career has he raced into the final laps of an event with a chance to win. But he's everything a PR-conscious sponsor wants—intelligent, articulate, pleasant, and polite around fans, willing to sign autographs and appear at public functions, and happy to promote the product.

ough/Donnie Allison donnybrook at the end of the 1979 Daytona 500 helped bring racing into national prominence.

NASCAR grew so upscale and accepted in the 1990s that it opened a marketing and public relations office on Park Avenue in midtown Manhattan. From there, it was only a short ride to Wall Street and Madison Avenue, and to the corporate headquarters of the major television networks. As the staff at NASCAR's ever-expanding headquarters in Daytona Beach prepared for the 1998 season, much of its work focused on marketing

new Texas Motor Speedway (TMS) in the Dallas-Fort Worth area debuted with a Busch/Cup doubleheader in 1997, but couldn't wrangle a second date for 1998. Likewise, Roger Penske's new track east of Los Angeles hosted Cup, Busch, and Craftsman races in 1997, but got only one Cup date (plus Busch and Craftsman races) for 1998. The new track at Las Vegas had a Craftsman Truck race in 1996, Craftsman and Busch races in 1997, and will have all three of NASCAR's top divisions in 1998.

The expansion into Southern California, New England, and Texas didn't come without a price. In 1996, after hosting stock car races since 1949, the North Wilkesboro Speedway in western North Carolina was sold for its dates. With his 50 percent share, Bahre moved one date to his NHIS for a fall race. And with his 50 percent share, Smith moved the other date to TMS for that track's inaugural spring race.

By the middle of the 1990s, Smith owned five active Winston Cup tracks and half of

LEFT AND BELOW: The pairing of driver Jeff Gordon and crew chief Ray Evernham has resulted in one of NASCAR's most successful and respected teams. They won the 1995 and 1997 Winston Cup, finished second to their teammate Terry Labonte in 1996, and started 1998 like they intended to make it three for four. Unlike most team sayings, the Rainbow Warriors' seems to fit right in: "Refuse to Lose."

Bobby Hamilton, who won two races with Petty Enterprises before moving to Morgan-McClure for the 1998 season.

Ricky Rudd leads the pack past
the sold-out frontstretch grand-
stand of the Charlotte Speedway
in the fall of 1995.

The father-son combination of
Robert (right) and Doug Yates is
part of the reason Robert Yates
Racing is so successful. Robert
Yates is among the alumni of Holman-Moody who "graduated" to
become respected engine
builders, crew chiefs, and team
owners. Yates bought his team
from Harry Ranier in 1988 and
had immediate success with
Davey Allison. Among Yates'
other drivers: Ernie Irvan (who
came in when Allison was killed),
Dale Jarrett (who came in when
Irvan was hurt), and 1998 Rookie
of the Year candidate Kenny
Irwin, who replaced Irvan after
the 1997 season.

North Wilkesboro Speedway. His empire included facilities near Charlotte; Dallas-Fort Worth; Atlanta; Sonoma, California; and Bristol, Tennessee. His Speedway Motorsports Inc. hosted eight Winston Cup races, plus The Winston Select All-Star race at Charlotte Motor Speedway. Not to be outdone, Bill France Jr. and his International Speedway Corp. (ISC) also held eight dates: two each at Talladega, Daytona Beach, and Darlington, and one each at Watkins Glen and Phoenix. In addition, ISC owns the Homestead (Florida) Motorsports Complex and is building a 1.5-mile speedway near Kansas City, Kansas.

Penske Motorsports Inc. was the other major player in the "how many tracks do you have?" game. His speedways at Brooklyn, Michigan, and Rockingham, North Carolina, got two Cup dates each, his new facility at Fontana, California, got one, and he is involved in the construction of a new track in Colorado. That left five men to control the other NASCAR tracks (and their remaining 11 dates): Paul Sawyer at Richmond, Virginia; Clay Earles at Martinsville, Virginia; John Rollins at Dover; Bahre in New Hampshire; Dr. Joe Matteoli at Pocono, Pennsylvania; and "newcomer" Richie Clyne at Las Vegas.

THE KING LEAVES AND THE SENSATION ARRIVES

The sport's most popular personality retired in the 1990s and his successor—if not in the people's heart, then certainly on the track—walked in at the same time. Richard Petty announced in the summer of 1991 that 1992 would be his last as a driver. His year-long farewell tour produced overflowing crowds to salute the man whose records for career starts, victories, smiles, and gracious autographs will never be broken.

"King Richard" may have lingered too long—his last victory was in 1984 and he'd struggled for most of the previous five years—and he wasn't the best at hiring replacements. By 1998, he'd gone through Rick Wilson, Wally Dallenbach, John Andretti, and Bobby Hamilton (who did win twice in his 94 starts), before rehiring Andretti after Hamilton quit after the 1997 season. But if fans thought Petty's retirement would leave a void, they were quickly proved wrong. On November 15, 1992, as Petty crashed and burned in the Hooters 500 at the Atlanta Motor Speedway (then came out of the garage in the final laps to be running at the finish), 20-year-old Jeff Gordon was making his Cup debut. Hardly anyone noticed his 31st-place finish, as Petty's final start dominated much of the local and national news.

It was perhaps the last time anyone overshadowed the man who became known as "Wonder Boy." Gordon was 14th in points and the 1993 Winston Cup Rookie of the

Ricky Craven, a former Busch Series star and 1995 Winston Cup Rookie of the Year. While the great majority of Winston Cup drivers are from the Southeast and Midwest, Craven is among the group of New England natives who've made a name in NASCAR. He advanced from the Busch North to the Busch Series, then drove for Larry Hedrick before getting a call from Rick Hendrick to join his team for the 1997 season. A series of wreck-related injuries put Craven's career on hold early in 1998.

Terry Labonte captured his second Winston Cup championship in 1996, 12 years after winning his first title. It was the longest stretch between championships in NASCAR history.

Never one to let a good publicity opportunity pass, Darrell Waltrip unveiled this pseudo-chrome Chevrolet for the 1995 Daytona 500.

Unlike Indy cars, sports cars, and drag racing, NASCAR-style stock car racing is marked by close no-quarter racing and ample contact. It's called by a variety of names: rootin', framming' and bammin', using the chrome horn, taking what's mine, or leaning. Occasionally seen on superspeedways, it's virtually the way of life at half-mile tracks where there's simply not enough room for all 43 highly-competitive drivers to put their cars at the front of the field. But since what goes around comes around (there is, after all, another race next weekend), drivers are quick to "apologize" when they feel they've gone over the line. (They may not mean it, but at least they make an effort.)

The infamous carburetor restrictor plate which limits how much fuel and air get through the carburetor and into the intake manifold of a Winston Cup car. The plate cuts horsepower, acceleration, and speed at Daytona Beach and Talladega.

Year. He won a 125-mile qualifier at Daytona Beach in February 1994, then won the Coca-Cola World 600, and the inaugural Brickyard 400 later that year. He was eighth in points in 1994, won the 1995 championship, and was second to teammate Terry Labonte in 1996, then won the 1997 championship. Clearly, he and crew chief Ray Evernham were the combination that seemed destined to lead NASCAR into the next millennium.

Gordon was among more than a dozen young drivers to make their mark in the 1990s. Andretti turned his back on Indy car racing to become a full-time NASCAR driver, a decision that looked good when he got his breakthrough victory in the July 1997, Pepsi 400 at the Daytona International Speedway. Johnny Benson came from the minor-league American Speed Association tour to become a Busch Series Rookie of the Year and series champion en route to a full-time ride in Winston Cup. Likewise, Hamilton, Jeff and Ward Burton, Ricky Craven, Kenny Wallace, David and Jeff Green, Robert Pressley, Bobby Labonte, Steve Grissom, Joe Nemechek, and Steve Park came through NASCAR's Busch Series to find a home in Winston Cup in the 1990s.

Petty, Buddy Baker, Jimmy Means, and Dick Brooks finally retired in the 1990s. Alan Kulwicki, the 1993 Winston

Cup champion, died in a plane crash in April 1994 and rising superstar Davey Allison was killed in a helicopter crash later that same year. Popular star Neil Bonnett died practicing for the 1994 Daytona 500, and 1989 Busch Series champion and 1990 Cup Rookie of the Year Rob Moroso died in a highway crash late in the 1990 season. And Bill France Sr., the man whose resolve, vision, and political savvy led to the creation and early growth of major-league stock car racing, died at his home in Ormond Beach, Florida, on June 7, 1992.

With its stock car tours as successful as they could be, NASCAR ventured into the world of pickup truck racing in 1994. It hosted a series of exhibitions in the Southwest and on the West Coast, then announced plans to support a full schedule in 1995. Mike Skinner won the inaugural Craftsman SuperTruck championship, Ron Hornaday won the second, and Jack Sprague the third. At mid-decade, it was evident the truck series had captured the imagination of long-time race fans and sponsors, and a new breed of fan—the urban cowboy who owns a pickup not because he needs it, but because it's the thing to have.

As usual, NASCAR knew exactly what it was doing.

The start of a NASCAR race never fails to bring the crowd to its feet. Almost every modern-day Winston Cup race is a sellout, but it wasn't always that way. As recently as the early 1990s, good tickets might be available on the day of the race, and scalpers were always trying to unload tickets in the parking lots. Now, even with more seats and the constant presence of TV, good seats are hard to come by even months before the event.

Michael Waltrip, Dale Earnhardt, and Rick Mast chase Rusty Wallace along the frontstretch of the North Carolina Motor Speedway in the spring of 1997.

PREVIOUS: There's always a moment of stirring patriotism and reverence before the start of each NASCAR race. This is just before the start of the February 1997 race at the North Carolina Motor Speedway near Rockingham.

Kyle Petty gets quick service from his crew during the spring 1998 race at the Darlington Raceway. After driving for others throughout the early part of his career, Lee's grandson and Richard's son left Team Sabco following the 1996 season and formed his own No. 44 Pontiac team. With two teenage sons coming along, it's obvious he's looking to give NASCAR its fourth-generation Petty in a Petty-owned car.

Jeff Burton came to Winston Cup after years in weekly short-track Late Model racing and on the touring Busch Grand National series.

OPPOSITE: Citgo leads McDonald's and Interstate Batteries into a turn. Or is it Michael Waltrip leading Bill Elliott and Bobby Labonte? In today's sponsorship-oriented environment it's often hard to tell whether NASCAR is a sport among men and machines or among competing sales reps. Part of this is because race fans are fiercely loyal, willing to stick with their favorite team through thick or thin and buying its sponsor's products. When "outsiders" question this alleged brand loyalty, sponsors have simply to roll out their "before and after" sales figures to prove their point.

Driver Dale Earnhardt and owner Richard Childress have been a formidable combination since teaming up in 1984.

Former Modified and Grand National star Jimmy Spencer now drives the Travis Carter-owned Ford sponsored by Winston, a long-time presence in NASCAR racing.

Dale Jarrett on his way to victory in the 400-mile race in the spring of 1998 at the Darlington Raceway. Jarrett is NASCAR's second most successful second-generation driver (Richard Petty is number one) and one of its brightest young stars. Young? He's 42 but didn't come into his own until the getting good equipment—the Wood Brothers, then Joe Gibbs Racing, then Robert Yates Racing—in the early 1990s. He hopes to join Richard Petty as the only other second-generation driver to win a championship after his father won one. Dale's father, Ned, won the 1961 and 1965 NASCAR titles.

John Andretti cast his racing lot with NASCAR after giving Indy car, sports car road racing, and even NHRA Top Fuel racing a look. He won the 1997 Pepsi 400 at Daytona Beach for Cale Yarborough Motorsports then moved to the Richard Petty-owned team for 1998.

Morgan Shepherd was picked to drive the No. 46, Felix Sabates-owned Chevrolet Monte Carlo after Wally Dallenbach left the team in the spring of 1998.

OPPOSITE TOP: Jeff Burton and his Jack Roush-owned, Exide-backed Ford team became a force in Winston Cup racing in 1997 when it won three races.

OPPOSITE BOTTOM: Lawyer-turned-racer Chad Little is typical of NASCAR's new breed: young, intelligent, well-spoken, and determined to be successful.

Bill Elliott and his self-owned, McDonald's-backed Ford. Even though he's been in something of a slump since leaving the Junior Johnson team in the mid-1990s, Elliott remains one of NASCAR's most popular drivers. His resume includes 49 poles and 40 victories—all but one of them on superspeedways—but no trips to victory lane since the 1994 Southern 500 at Darlington. He won the inaugural Winston Million in 1985 and the Winston Cup championship in 1988.

Darlington Raceway has been hosting Winston Cup races since its inaugural Southern 500 in 1950. It remains one of the toughest tracks NASCAR visits because each end of the speedway is dramatically different from the other. Drivers and chassis experts know they can't master both ends of the track, so they give up something at one end—each team has its own preference—in order to be strong at the other. They use spring rubbers, adjust track bars, and change the air pressure in their tires to accommodate the ever-changing track conditions.

APPENDICES

Close-quarters racing continues to be a part of NASCAR racing, which probably has something to do with its popularity. Rusty Wallace leads a freight train of big names, with Mark Martin, Jeff Gordon, and Dale Earnhardt in hot pursuit.

Year-By-Year Summary

1949 SEASON: eight races between June 19 at Charlotte, North Carolina, and October 16 at North Wilkesboro, North Carolina; no driver made all eight starts, but eight of the 50 who scored points started six; Sara Christian, the first woman to compete in what would become Winston Cup, finished 13th in points; the 1949 champion was Red Byron of Atlanta, who won twice; other winners that season: Bob Flock also won two, and Lee Petty, Curtis Turner, Jim Roper, and Jack White one each.

1950 SEASON: 51 races between February 5 at Daytona Beach, Florida, and October 29 at Hillsborough, North Carolina, including the inaugural Southern 500 at Darlington on September 4; Bill Rexford started 17 of the 19 races and won the championship with one victory and 10 additional top-10 finishes; 51 drivers earned points, and there were 14 winners: Curtis Turner won four, Dick Linder three, and Rexford, Fireball Roberts, Lee Petty, Lloyd Moore, Johnny Mantz, Jimmy Florian, Bill Blair, Herb Thomas, Fonty Flock, Tim Flock, Leon Sales, and Harold Kite won one each.

1951 SEASON: 41 races between February 11 at Daytona Beach, Florida, and November 25 at Mobile, Alabama; for the first time, NASCAR hosted races in California and Arizona; Herb Thomas, Fonty Flock, and his brother, Tim, finished 1-2-3 in points after each started 33 races—the most starts that season; Fonty Flock won eight of them, Thomas and Tim Flock seven each; Frank Mundy won three; and Lee Petty, Bob Flock, Tommy Thompson, Lou Figaro, Danny Weinberg, Neil Cole, Bill Norton, and Marvin Burke one each.

1952 SEASON: 34 races between January 20 at West Palm Beach, Florida, and November 30 at the same venue; Tim Flock, Herb Thomas, and Lee Petty were 1-2-3 in points and combined for 19 victories; Flock and Thomas each won eight, and Petty three; other winners included Dick Rathmann with five, Fonty Flock and Marshall Teague with two, and Bill Blair, Donald Thomas, Buddy Shuman, Gober Sosebee, and Buck Baker one each.

1953 SEASON: 37 races between February 1 at West Palm Beach, Florida, and November 1 at Atlanta; Herb Thomas, Lee Petty, and Dick Rathmann were 1-2-3 in points, with Thomas

Here's a scene familiar to race fans in 1967—Richard Petty on his way to victory lane. Petty set untouchable records with 27 victories, including 10 in a row. Here, Petty and "Johnny Reb" are headed for victory lane after the 1967 Southern 500 at Darlington Raceway.

the only driver to run all 37 races; he won 12, Petty and Rathmann won five each, Buck Baker and Fonty Flock won four each, Speedy Thompson won two, and Tim Flock, Jim Paschal, Bill Blair, Dick Passwater, and Curtis Turner one each.

1954 SEASON: 37 races between February 7 at West Palm Beach, Florida, and October 24 at North Wilkesboro, North Carolina; Lee Petty, Herb Thomas, and Buck Baker finished 1-2-3 in points; each ran 34 races; Thomas won 12, Petty seven, Buck Baker and West Coast newcomer Hershel McGriff each won four; the rest were divided among Dick Rathmann (three), Al Keller (two) and Jim Paschal, Curtis Turner, Gober Sosebee, Danny Letner, and John Soares, each with one victory.

1955 SEASON: 45 races between November 7, 1954, at High Point, North Carolina, and October 30, 1955, at Hillsborough, North Carolina; Buck Baker and Lee Petty ran 42 of them, but finished second and third in points to champion Tim Flock,

who started only 38; Flock won 18 to Petty's six and Baker's three; Junior Johnson won five, Fonty Flock, Herb Thomas, and Jim Paschal three each, Speedy Thompson two, and Norm Nelson, George Parris, and Danny Letner one.

1956 SEASON: 56 races between October 30, 1955, at Hickory, North Carolina, and November 18, 1956, at Wilson, North Carolina; Buck Baker and Herb Thomas started 48 (more than any other drivers) and finished 1-2 in points; Baker won 14, third-ranked Speedy Thompson eight, and Thomas and Fireball Roberts five each; other winners: Tim Flock and Ralph Moody with four, Lee Petty, Billy Myers, and Lloyd Dane with two, and Fonty Flock, John Kiepler, Eddie Pagan, Jack Smith, Curtis Turner, Paul Goldsmith, Marvin Panch, and Jim Paschal, each with one.

1957 SEASON: 53 races between November 11, 1956, at Lancaster, California, and October, 27, 1957, at Greensboro, North Carolina; Buck Baker, Marvin Panch, and Speedy

Thompson were 1-2-3 in points, although none of them ran the full schedule; Baker won 10 of 40 starts, Panch six of 42, and Thompson two of 38; Fireball Roberts won eight races, and Paul Goldsmith, Lee Petty, and Jack Smith each won four; other winners included Eddie Pagan with three, Gwyn Staley with two, and Cotton Owens, Ralph Moody, Bill Amick, Lloyd Dane, Danny Graves, Art Watts, Parnelli Jones, Bob Welborn, and Marvin Porter with one each.

1958 SEASON: 51 races between November 3, 1957, at Fayetteville, North Carolina, and October 26, 1958, at Atlanta; Lee Petty ran 50 of the 51 and won the championship over Buck Baker and Speedy Thompson; Petty won a series-high seven races, followed by Junior Johnson and Fireball Roberts with six, Bob Welborn with five, Thompson and Jim Reed with four, and Baker and Curtis Turner with three; Jack Smith and Rex White won two, with Eddie Gray, Paul Goldsmith, Jim Paschal, Parnelli Jones, Joe Eubanks, Frankie Schneider, Joe Weatherly, Cotton Owens, and Shorty Rollins (NASCAR's first Rookie of the Year), each won once.

1959 SEASON: 44 races between November 11, 1958, at Fayetteville, North Carolina, and October 25, 1959, at Concord, North Carolina; Lee Petty won 11 races (including the first Daytona 500) and the last of his three championships, beating Cotton Owens and Speedy Thompson; Jack Smith, Red White, and Junior Johnson each won five and Jim Reed won three; two-time winners were Tom Pistone, Bob Welborn, Ned Jarrett, and Curtis Turner; single wins went to Owens, Parnelli Jones, Joe Lee Johnson, Buck Baker, Eddie Gray, Fireball Roberts, and Johnny Beauchamp, runner-up in the first Daytona 500.

1960 SEASON: 44 races between November 8, 1959, at Charlotte, North Carolina, and October 30, 1960, at Hampton, Georgia; with six victories in 42 starts, Rex White easily won the championship ahead of newcomers Richard Petty and Bobby Johns; Ned Jarrett, Junior Johnson, and Lee Petty each won five races, and Junior Johnson, Jack Smith, Fireball Roberts, and Joe Weatherly each won two; the other victories were divided one each among Johns, Johnny Beauchamp, Joe Lee Johnson, Cotton Owens, Jim Cook, and John Rostek; the first of Richard Petty's record 200 victories came on February 28 on a half-mile dirt track in Charlotte, North Carolina.

1961 SEASON: 52 races between November 6, 1960, at Charlotte, North Carolina, and October 29, 1961, at Hillsborough, North Carolina; one-time winner Ned Jarrett won the first of his two NASCAR championships ahead of seven-time winner Rex White and two-time winner Emanuel Zervakis; Joe Weatherly led the series with nine victories, Junior Johnson won

seven, Cotton Owens four, and Fred Lorenzen and David Pearson three each; two-time winners were Jack Smith, Richard Petty, Jim Paschal, Fireball Roberts, and Eddie Gray; Buck Baker, Nelson Stacy, Marvin Panch, Bob Burdick, Lloyd Dane, and Lee Petty each won one.

1962 SEASON: 53 races between November 5, 1961, at Concord, North Carolina, and October 28, 1962, at Hampton, Georgia; Joe Weatherly won the first of his two driving titles with a series-leading nine victories; Richard Petty won eight times and finished second in points, while third-ranked Ned Jarrett won six races; Rex White won eight races, Jack Smith five, Jim Paschal four, and Fireball Roberts and Nelson Stacy three each; Fred Lorenzen won twice, with single victories going to Cotton Owens, Bobby Johns, Jimmy Pardue, Johnny Allen, Larry Frank, and Junior Johnson.

1963 SEASON: 55 races between November 4, 1962, at Birmingham, Alabama, and November 3, 1963, at Riverside, California; Joe Weatherly won three races in 53 starts, but still won the championship ahead of 14-time winner Richard Petty and six-time winner Fred Lorenzen; Ned Jarrett won eight races, Junior Johnson seven, Jim Paschal five, and Fireball Roberts four; eight other drivers each won once: Jimmy Pardue, Darel Dieringer, Tiny Lund, Buck Baker, Marvin Panch, Dan Gurney, Johnny Rutherford, and Glen Wood.

1964 SEASON: 62 races between November 10, 1963, at Concord, North Carolina, and November 8, 1964, at Jacksonville, North Carolina; the longest season in NASCAR history saw Richard Petty win the first of his seven titles; Ned Jarrett and David Pearson finished second and third; Petty won nine races, six fewer than Jarrett and one more than Pearson; Fred Lorenzen also won eight, Billy Wade won four (consecutively, in the month of July), and Junior Johnson and Marvin Panch won three; veteran Buck Baker and newcomer LeeRoy Yarborough won two each, and single victories went to Jim Paschal, Darel Dieringer, Wendell Scott (the only African-American to win a major stock car race), Bobby Isaac, Dan Gurney, A.J. Foyt, Cotton Owens, and Fireball Roberts; Weatherly and Roberts were killed while racing, and Jimmy Pardue was killed in a tire-testing accident.

1965 SEASON: 55 races between January 17, 1965, at Riverside, California, and November 7, 1965, at Moyock, North Carolina; Ned Jarrett won 13 races and his second NASCAR championship, this one ahead of newcomer (and nine-time winner) Dick Hutcherson and one-time winner Darel Dieringer; Junior Johnson won 13 races, but didn't run enough to contend for the title; Richard Petty, Fred Lorenzen, and Marvin Panch each won four races, and David Pearson won two; single victories

Pete Hamilton in the No. 1 King Enterprises Dodge and Bobby Allison in the No. 2 car on the pace lap at the Southern 500.

went to Dan Gurney, Tiny Lund, A.J. Foyt, Curtis Turner, and a promising young driver named Cale Yarborough.

1966 SEASON: 49 races between November 14, 1965, at Augusta, Georgia, and October 30, 1966, at Rockingham, North Carolina; David Pearson won 15 races and his first championship ahead of winless James Hylton and eight-time winner Richard Petty; Paul Goldsmith, Dick Hutcherson, Darel Dieringer, and newcomer Bobby Allison each won three times; Fred Lorenzen, Elmo Langley, and Jim Paschal each won two, with Earl Balmer, Dan Gurney, Jim Hurtubise, Marvin Panch, Tiny Lund, Sam McQuagg, Paul Lewis, and LeeRoy Yarbrough each winning one race.

1967 SEASON: 49 races between November 13, 1966, at Augusta, Georgia, and November 5, 1967, at Weaverville, North Carolina; in the most dominating performance in NASCAR history, Richard Petty won 27 races, including 10 consecutively late in the season; he easily won the championship ahead of winless James Hylton and two-race winner Dick Hutcherson; Bobby Allison won six times, Jim Paschal four, and Cale Yarborough and David Pearson two each; Parnelli Jones won once, as did LeeRoy Yarbrough, Mario Andretti (the Daytona 500), Fred Lorenzen, Darel Dieringer, and Buddy Baker.

1968 SEASON: 49 races between November 12, 1967, at Macon, Georgia, and November 3, 1968, at Jefferson, Georgia; David Pearson won 16 races and his second NASCAR championship ahead of three-time winner Bobby Isaac; Richard Petty also won 16 races, but didn't run enough to challenge Pearson for the title; Cale Yarborough won six races, Bobby Isaac four, and Bobby Allison two; Dan Gurney, Buddy Baker, Donnie Allison, LeeRoy Yarbrough, and Charlie Glotzbach were one-time winners.

1969 SEASON: 54 races between November 17, 1968, at Macon, Georgia, and December 7, 1969, at College Station, Texas; David Pearson won his second consecutive championship and third in the past four years; he won 11 races, six fewer than Bobby Isaac, who was sixth in points; second-ranked Richard Petty won 10 races and LeeRoy Yarbrough seven; Bobby Allison won four, Cale Yarborough two, and Richard Brickhouse and Donnie Allison one each.

1970 SEASON: 48 races between January 1 at Riverside, California, and November 22 at Hampton, Virginia; after being one of the sport's dominant drivers for several years, Bobby Isaac finally won the championship ahead of Bobby Allison and James Hylton; Richard Petty won 18 races and Isaac 11, the only drivers in double-figures; Donnie Allison, Bobby Allison, Pete Hamilton, and Cale Yarborough each won three, Charlie Glotzbach won two, and Hylton, A.J. Foyt, David Pearson, Buddy Baker, and LeeRoy Yarbrough one each.

1971 SEASON: 48 races between January 10 at Riverside, California, and December 12 at College Station, Texas; in the last of NASCAR's "long seasons," Richard Petty won 21 races and his third championship ahead of James Hylton and Cecil Gordon; Bobby Allison won 11 races, Bobby Isaac four, and A.J. Foyt, Tiny Lund, and David Pearson two each; single victories went to Ray Elder, Pete Hamilton, Buddy Baker, Benny Parsons, Donnie Allison, and Charlie Glotzbach.

1972 SEASON: 31 races between January 23 at Riverside, California, and November 12 at College Station, Texas; the first of NASCAR's "modern seasons" saw Richard Petty win the championship over Bobby Allison and James Hylton; Allison led the tour with 10 victories to Petty's eight and the six of David Pearson; A.J. Foyt and Buddy Baker each won two races, and Hylton, Bobby Isaac, and Ray Elder one each.

1973 SEASON: 28 races between January 12 at Riverside, California, and October 21 at Rockingham, North Carolina; Benny Parsons won the championship with only one victory, 10 fewer than David Pearson, who ran a limited schedule and didn't contest the championship; Richard Petty won six races, Cale Yarborough four, Buddy Baker and Bobby Allison two, and Parsons, Mark Donohue, and Dick Brooks one each.

1974 SEASON: 30 races between January 26 at Riverside, California, and November 24 at Ontario, California.; Richard Petty and Cale Yarborough each won 10 races, but Petty won the championship over Yarborough and seven-time winner David Pearson; Bobby Allison won twice and Earl Ross once.

1975 SEASON: 30 races between January 19 at Riverside, California, and November 23 at Ontario, California; 13-race winner Richard Petty won his sixth championship ahead of one-time winner Dave Marcis and winless James Hylton; Buddy Baker won four races, Bobby Allison, Cale Yarborough, and David Pearson three each, and newcomer Darrell Waltrip won two; single victories went to Marcis and Benny Parsons.

1976 SEASON: 30 races between January 18 at Riverside, California, and November 21 at Ontario, California; Cale Yarborough won nine races and the first of his three consecutive championships, this one ahead of Richard Petty and Benny Parsons; David Pearson won 10 races (but didn't contest the full schedule) and Petty and Dave Marcis won three

each; Parsons won two, and Darrell Waltrip, Donnie Allison, and Buddy Baker one each.

1977 SEASON: 30 races between January 16 at Riverside, California and November 20 at Ontario, California; Cale Yarborough won nine races and the championship, once again ahead of Richard Petty and Benny Parsons; Darrell Waltrip won six races, Petty five, and Parsons four; David Pearson, Neil Bonnett, and Donnie Allison won two each.

1978 SEASON: 30 races between January 22 at Riverside, California, and November 19 at Ontario, California; Cale Yarborough won 10 races and easily beat five-time winner Bobby Allison and six-time winner Darrell Waltrip for the championship; David Pearson won four and Benny Parsons three; Donnie Allison and Lennie Pond won one each; Richard Petty was winless for the first time since 1959.

1979 SEASON: 31 races between January 14 at Riverside, California, and November 18 at Ontario, California; Richard Petty won five races and the last of his seven championships, beating seven-race winner Darrell Waltrip and five-race winner Bobby Allison; Cale Yarborough won four times, Buddy Baker and Neil Bonnett three, and Benny Parsons two; David Pearson and newcomer Dale Earnhardt each won once.

1980 SEASON: 31 races between January 19 at Riverside, California, and November 15 at Ontario, California; Dale Earnhardt became the first driver to be Rookie of the Year one season and champion the next, winning five races and edging Cale Yarborough and Darrell Waltrip for the title; Yarborough won six races, Waltrip five, Bobby Allison four, Benny Parsons three, and Richard Petty, Neil Bonnett, and Buddy Baker two each; single wins went to Terry Labonte and David Pearson, his 105th and final in Winston Cup.

1981 SEASON: 31 races between January 11 at Riverside, California, and November 22 at the same venue; the first of Darrell Waltrip's three championships came over Bobby Allison and Harry Gant; with 12 victories, Waltrip easily dominated the season; Allison won five, Richard Petty, Benny Parsons, and Neil Bonnett three each, and Cale Yarborough won two; Jody Ridley, Morgan Shepherd, and Ron Bouchard each won once.

1982 SEASON: 30 races between January 14 at Daytona Beach, Florida, and November 21 at Riverside, California; after 12 years of opening the season on the West Coast, NASCAR moved its opener to Daytona International Speedway; Waltrip won his second consecutive title, this one over Bobby Allison and Terry Labonte; Waltrip won 12 races, Allison eight, Cale

Yarborough three, Harry Gant and Tim Richmond two; Dave Marcis, Dale Earnhardt, and Neil Bonnett won one each.

1983 SEASON: 30 races between February 20 at Daytona Beach, Florida, and November 20 at Riverside, California; after years of trying and so many heartbreaks, Bobby Allison finally won his only Winston Cup over Darrell Waltrip and Bill Elliott; Allison and Waltrip each won six races, Cale Yarborough won four, Richard Petty three, and Neil Bonnett, Dale Earnhardt, and Ricky Rudd two each; one-time winners were Elliott, Buddy Baker, Harry Gant, Terry Labonte, and Tim Richmond.

1984 SEASON: 30 races between February 19 at Daytona Beach, Florida, and November 18 at Riverside, California; Terry Labonte won two races and the first of his two NASCAR championships, beating three-race winners Harry Gant and Bill Elliott; Darrell Waltrip won seven times, Geoff Bodine and Cale Yarborough won three, Bobby Allison, Dale Earnhardt, and Richard Petty won twice (including his 200th and final victory); Benny Parsons, Ricky Rudd, and Tim Richmond each won once.

1985 SEASON: 28 races between February 17 at Daytona Beach, Florida, and November 28 at Riverside, California, the shortest schedule in 35 years because both Nashville, Tennessee, races were dropped; Darrell Waltrip won only three times, but out-pointed 11-race winner Bill Elliott and three-race winner Harry Gant for the championship; Dale Earnhardt won four races; Neil Bonnett and Cale Yarborough won two; Terry Labonte, Ricky Rudd, and Greg Sacks one each.

1986 SEASON: 29 races between February 16 at Daytona Beach, Florida, and November 16 at Riverside, California, including a return to Watkins Glen, New York, after a 19-year break; six years after his first title, Dale Earnhardt won his second; he had five victories, two fewer than third-ranked Tim Richmond; second-ranked Darrell Waltrip won three races; Rusty Wallace, Ricky Rudd, Geoff Bodine, and Bill Elliott won two; single-race winners were Terry Labonte, Bobby Hillin, Morgan Shepherd, Kyle Petty, Neil Bonnett, and Bobby Allison.

1987 SEASON: 29 races between February 15 at Daytona Beach, Florida, and November 29 at Hampton, Georgia, the first time the season had ended in the Southeast since the 1973

Rockingham finale; Dale Earnhardt won 11 races and his third title, this one over six-race winner Bill Elliott and one-time winner Terry Labonte; Davey Allison, Ricky Rudd, Tim Richmond, and Rusty Wallace each won two; Darrell Waltrip, Kyle Petty, and Bobby Allison won one each.

1988 SEASON: 29 races between February 14 at Daytona Beach, Florida, and November 29 at Hampton, Georgia; Bill Elliott won six races and his first championship over six-race winner Rusty Wallace and three-race winner Dale Earnhardt; Neil Bonnett, Davey Allison, and Darrell Waltrip each won twice; a host of drivers won one race: Alan Kulwicki, Ricky Rudd, Ken Schrader, Geoff Bodine, Lake Speed, Phil Parsons, Terry Labonte, and Bobby Allison, whose Daytona 500 victory came six months before a career-ending injury at Pocono, Pennsylvania.

1989 SEASON: 29 races between February 19 at Daytona Beach, Florida, and November 19 at Hampton, Georgia; a new mid-summer race at Sonoma, California, replaced the summer race at Riverside, California, where the Riverside International Raceway was closing down after hosting Winston Cup races since 1963; six-race winner Rusty Wallace won the championship over five-race winner Dale Earnhardt by 12 points, one of the closest championship battles in Winston Cup history; one-race winner Mark Martin, six-race winner Darrell Waltrip, and one-race winner Ken Schrader rounded out the top-5 in points; Bill Elliott won three races, Terry Labonte and Davey Allison two each; Harry Gant, Ricky Rudd, and Geoff Bodine won one each. The season-ender at Atlanta International Raceway saw Earnhardt win the race and Wallace the championship, both events overshadowed by the death of veteran driver Grant Adcox in a single-car accident.

1990 SEASON: 29 races between February 18 at Daytona Beach, Florida, and November 18 at Hampton, Georgia; Dale Earnhardt beat Mark Martin by 26 points for the championship, with third-place Geoff Bodine well behind; Earnhardt won nine races, Martin and Bodine three each; Greg Sacks, Rusty Wallace, and Davey Allison two each; one-time winners were Kyle Petty, Brett Bodine, Ricky Rudd, Harry Gant, Ernie Irvan, Morgan Shepherd, Alan Kulwicki, and Bill Elliott.

1991 SEASON: 29 races between February 17 at Daytona Beach, Florida, and November 17 at Hampton, Georgia; Dale Earnhardt won his fifth championship, this one over Ricky Rudd and Davey Allison; with five victories each, Allison and

David Pearson's banged-up car in victory lane after he and Richard Petty crashed on the last lap. Petty wound up in the grass with a dead motor, while Pearson limped across the finish line to win the 1976 Daytona 500.

Harry Gant led the series; Earnhardt won four; Darrell Waltrip, Ernie Irvan, Ken Schrader, and Rusty Wallace won two each; Rudd won once, as did Bill Elliott, Alan Kulwicki, Dale Jarrett, Mark Martin, and Kyle Petty.

1992 SEASON: 29 races between February 16 at Daytona Beach, Florida, and November 15 at Hampton, Georgia; two-race winner Alan Kulwicki won the championship by 10 points over five-race winner Bill Elliott and by 63 points over five-race winner Davey Allison; Ernie Irvan and Darrell Waltrip each won three times; Harry Gant, Geoff Bodine, Mark Martin, and Kyle Petty won two each; Dale Earnhardt, Ricky Rudd, and Rusty Wallace each won once; it was the final season for seven-time champion and 200-race winner Richard Petty.

1993 SEASON: 30 races between February 14 at Daytona Beach, Florida, and November 14 at Hampton, Georgia; the new venue was the New Hampshire International Speedway, a one-mile facility near Loudon; Dale Earnhardt won six races and the championship over 10-race winner Rusty Wallace and five-race winner Mark Martin; Geoff Bodine won three times, and everyone else once each: Davey Allison, Geoff Bodine, Ricky Rudd, Dale Jarrett, Kyle Petty, and Morgan Shepherd; tragedy struck as defending series champion Alan Kulwicki and rising superstar Davey Allison died in separate air crashes.

1994 SEASON: 31 races between February 20 in Daytona Beach, Florida, and November 13 at Hampton, Georgia; the new venue was the Indianapolis Motor Speedway, which hosted the inaugural Brickyard 400 in August; Dale Earnhardt beat Mark Martin and Rusty Wallace for the championship, his record-tying seventh; Wallace won eight races; Earnhardt four; Ernie Irvan, Terry Labonte, and Geoff Bodine three; Martin and breakthrough winners Jimmy Spencer and Jeff Gordon won two each; single victories went to Ricky Rudd, Sterling Marlin, Bill Elliott, and Dale Jarrett.

1995 SEASON: 31 races between February 19 at Daytona Beach, Florida, and November 12 at Hampton, Georgia; Jeff Gordon won the championship with seven victories, two more than series runner-up Dale Earnhardt and four more than third-ranked Sterling Marlin; Mark Martin won four races; Terry Labonte and his brother, Bobby Labonte, each won three (they were the first of Bobby's career); Rusty Wallace won two; one-race winners were Ricky Rudd, Ward Burton (the first of his career), Kyle Petty, and Dale Jarrett.

1996 SEASON: 31 races between February 18 at Daytona Beach, Florida, and November 10 at Hampton, Georgia; Terry Labonte won only twice, but got his second championship ahead of teammate (and 10-time winner) Jeff Gordon and third-ranked and four-race winner Dale Jarrett; Rusty Wallace won five races; Dale Earnhardt and Sterling Marlin two each; and Geoff Bodine, Ricky Rudd, Bobby Hamilton (the first of his career), and Bobby Labonte were each one-time winners; after hosting NASCAR races since 1949, the North Wilkesboro (North Carolina) Speedway ran its last Cup race in September.

1997 SEASON: 32 races between February 16 at Daytona Beach, Florida, and November 16 at Hampton, Georgia; in place of the two North Wilkesboro races, the tour went to new tracks: Texas Motor Speedway and California Speedway, and added a second race at New Hampshire International Speedway; Jeff Gordon won 10 races and his second series championship, this one by 14 points over seven-race winner Dale Jarrett and by 22 points over four-race winner Mark Martin; Jeff Burton (three wins, the first of his career) and winless Dale Earnhardt (his first winless full season) rounded out the top-5 in points; Ricky Rudd won twice; John Andretti, Terry Labonte, Ernie Irvan, Rusty Wallace, and Bobby Hamilton each won once.

APPENDIX

B

Heroes

BOBBY ALLISON: Perhaps nobody gave more to stock car racing and suffered so much from it. An enormously popular driver, he began racing in 1961 and didn't quit until a horrific, life-threatening accident at Pocono, Pennsylvania, in the summer of 1988 ended his career and left him scarred for life. He made 717 starts, won 57 poles, and 84 races, and got slightly more than $7 million in official earnings. He won three Driver of the Year awards, was voted Most Popular Driver eight times, won the 1983 Winston Cup, and finished among the top-10 in points 17 other times. But his sons, Clifford and Davey, both died at race tracks, contributing to the breakup of his marriage, and the gradual collapse of the mid-pack Winston Cup team he started after realizing he'd never race again.

BUCK BAKER: One of stock car racing's earliest stars, Baker won 48 races and 44 poles in a career that spanned the 1950s, 1960s, and into the early 1970s. He won the 1956 and 1957 championships for owner Carl Kiekhaefer, and won three Southern 500s (1953, 1960, and 1964) for three different owners. He was among the pioneers in the ill-fated Grand American series in the late 1960s and early 1970s. His son, Buddy Baker, was the first NASCAR driver to run more than 200 miles per hour.

BUDDY BAKER: Elzie Wylie Baker Jr., better known as Buddy, was a master of super-speedway racing. Buck Baker's son won only 19 races in 698 starts, but among them were four each at Talladega and Charlotte, two each at Darlington, Daytona Beach, and Atlanta, and one each at Michigan, Ontario, and College Station, plus short track victories at Nashville and Martinsville. He retired in the early 1990s and became a thoroughly entertaining—if not professionally polished—television commentator.

HAROLD BRASINGTON: There wasn't a paved superspeedway in the South until he built Darlington Raceway in time for a Labor Day race in 1950. The inaugural Southern 500 was the first 500-mile race for stock cars, and it added credibility to Bill France's efforts to establish the series. Before he turned to promoting, Brasington was an accomplished driver, often racing against France in the 1930s on the highway/beach course

ABOVE: Ward Burton (left) and his brother Jeff are friendly rivals on and off the track. They moved in similar paths from weekly short-track racing in Virginia to the Busch Series, then to Winston Cup in the mid-1990s. Although Ward won first, Jeff won three times in 1997 and seems to be on the faster track.

Bobby Allison is one of the great names in NASCAR.

Davey Allison.

south of Daytona Beach. He got his inspiration for the track after seeing the financial impact of the tremendous crowds for the Indianapolis 500.

BLOYS BRITT: Long-time Associated Press sportswriter who was among the first to recognize the growing importance of stock car racing.

RED BYRON: In a short and sweet career, this decorated World War II veteran won the first NASCAR championship in 1949 for owner Raymond Parks, then raced only a few more years. He won on the Daytona Beach highway/road course and at Martinsville Speedway that first year, but was stripped of all points early in the 1950 season for running non-NASCAR events.

L. G. DEWITT: Twice during his career this mild-mannered, soft-spoken North Carolina businessman rode to the rescue of struggling speedways. He was there to help the North Carolina Motor Speedway at Rockingham when problems arose in the mid-1960s, then appeared in the late 1970s when Atlanta International Raceway needed financial and organizational help. He also owned a Winston Cup team in the early 1970s that won the 1973 Winston Cup championship and the 1975 Daytona 500 with driver Benny Parsons.

CLAY EARLES: One of NASCAR's most popular promoters built the half-mile Martinsville Speedway in 1947, and has been involved in its daily operation ever since. A long-time friend of Bill France Sr., he was the first short-track promoter to pave his facility, bucking conventional wisdom of the early 1950s that said dirt was better. He was always well ahead of fellow short-track promoters when it came to purses, spectator amenities, the upkeep of his facility, and promoting and advertising his events.

BILL ELLIOTT: Nicknamed "Awesome Bill" early in his career and "Dollar Bill" after winning the inaugural Winston Million in 1985. He came out of the Georgia backwoods in the late 1970s, struggled for a few years in his own cars, then began winning after joining with Michigan-based team owner Harry Melling. The relationship produced 34 victories (33 on super-speedways) between 1983 and 1991, when Bill left to drive for Junior Johnson. That union produced only six victories in 90 starts, so Elliott returned home to reopen his family-run team. He was the 1988 Winston Cup champion, is an unprecedented 12-time Most Popular Driver, and was the 1985 and 1988 American Driver of the Year. Still holds the all-time NASCAR qualifying record of 212.809, set at Talladega, Alabama, in 1985.

TIM FLOCK: One of three racing brothers from the Atlanta area (the other two were Bob and Fonty) who raced in the late 1940s and into the 1950s. He won 37 poles and 40 races, and the 1952 and 1955 series championships. When he retired in the late 1950s, though, he still wasn't up to $200,000 in career earnings. Fell ill in the winter of 1998, and died several months later of cancer.

BILL FRANCE SR.: Founder, long-time president, and guiding force in the birth and growth of major-league stock car racing. He was a skilled and successful racer in the 1930s before turning to promoting races and organizing the sanctioning body in the late 1940s. He built the super-fast speedways in Daytona Beach and Talladega, and helped bring big-time stock car racing to almost every corner of the country. He retired in 1972 and died in 1992 at his long-time home at Ormond Beach, Florida. Father of current NASCAR president Bill France Jr. and vice-president Jim France.

PETE HAMILTON: Raced with NASCAR for only a handful of years and made only 64 starts, but was the 1968 Rookie of the

Buck Baker was one of NASCAR's true pioneering legends. He raced in the 1940s, 1950s, 1960s, 1970s, and 1980s, winning 46 races and the 1956 and 1957 championships.

Year and won four high-profile races: the Daytona 500 and both Talladega races in 1970, and a Daytona 125-miler in 1971. He was among the first college graduates to drive in NASCAR and, some feel (records are vague about such things), the first college graduate to win a Winston Cup race.

RICK HENDRICK: Few owners who never raced themselves have been as successful as this multi-millionaire automobile magnate from Charlotte. He started Hendrick Motorsports in 1984 with Geoff Bodine and crew chief Harry Hyde, and promptly won three races. His record after 14 years showed 74 poles and 60 victories spread among seven drivers: Bodine, Tim Richmond, Darrell Waltrip, Ken Schrader, Ricky Rudd, Jeff Gordon, and Terry Labonte. Among Hendrick Motorsports' most impressive accomplishments: Winston Cup championships in 1995, 1996, and 1997, two victories in the Daytona 500, four in the Coca-Cola World 600, four in the Southern 500, and the inaugural Brickyard 400 in 1994. Hendrick Motorsports has also won two Winston all-star races, four Busch Clashes, and the 1997 Winston Million with Gordon.

DICK HUTCHERSON: One of a handful of drivers who came from Iowa in the 1950s and 1960s to race with NASCAR. His brother, Ron, was another, along with Tiny Lund, and Ramo Stott. A skilled dirt-track driver, Dick won 22 poles and 14 races between 1964 and his retirement after the 1968 season. He won only one superspeedway race—in 1965 at Atlanta—and half of his victories were on dirt tracks. He was second to Ned Jarrett in the 1965 championship standings, and third behind Richard Petty and James Hylton in the 1967 points.

NED JARRETT: This 1961 and 1965 champion won 35 poles and 50 races in only 351 career starts, including superspeedway

victories at Atlanta and Darlington. He retired in his mid 30s, well before the series took off and became national in scope. He's better known in the past 15 years as an outstanding radio and television commentator and the father of driver Dale Jarrett and television commentator Glen Jarrett. Ned is generally acknowledged as one of the most PR-conscious and gentlemanly drivers from NASCAR's early years.

JUNIOR JOHNSON: Author Thomas Wolfe called him "the last American hero," but long-time NASCAR fans remember him best as a no-mercy driver and later as a slick and successful team owner. After serving hard time in the 1950s for bootlegging, he turned to organized oval-track racing in 1953. He raced only 13 years, but won 47 poles and 50 races in 313 career starts with two dozen owners, including himself. His best season was 1965, when he won 13 of 36 races with owner Rex Lovette. Among his major victories: two each at Charlotte, Martinsville, and North Wilkesboro, and one each at Atlanta, Bristol, Darlington, Daytona Beach, and Richmond. Because he retired in 1966, he never raced on many of the tracks that make up today's series.

CARL KIEKHAEFER: He was the Rick Hendrick of his time—and his time was the 1950s. A wealthy Wisconsin businessman, Kiekhaefer had a major national sponsor at a time when most sponsors were corner garages or cafes. He fielded multi-car teams and won NASCAR championships with Tim Flock in 1955 and Buck Baker in 1956. He often fielded three team cars in races and once had his name and sponsorship on seven at one time. He demanded much from his drivers, which led to fairly high turnover. He stayed in NASCAR for only two years, but made an enormous impact while he was there.

FRED LORENZEN: The original "Golden Boy" came to NASCAR in the early 1960s from near Chicago, hardly the best training ground for stock car racing. But he won on both short tracks and long, and on paved and dirt tracks. All told, he won 33 poles and 26 races in 158 starts, all but a handful of them in the 1960s. (Better percentage than Yarborough who was noted above.) Among his notable victories: five at Martinsville, four each at Atlanta and Charlotte, three at Bristol, two at Darlington, and one each at Daytona Beach, Rockingham, and North Wilkesboro.

BUD MOORE: One of the most popular and enduring owners in NASCAR came home from World War II with a chest full of medals for bravery. After years preparing cars for minor-league series in the South, he went Winston Cup racing in 1961 with Joe Weatherly. They were fourth in points that year, then won the championship in 1962. Moore has fielded cars for some of NASCAR's all-time greats: Weatherly, Darel Dieringer, Buddy Baker, Bobby Allison, Benny Parsons, Dale Earnhardt, Ricky Rudd, and Geoff and Brett Bodine. He was versatile enough to dominate the Trans-Am series in 1969, 1970, and 1971, before

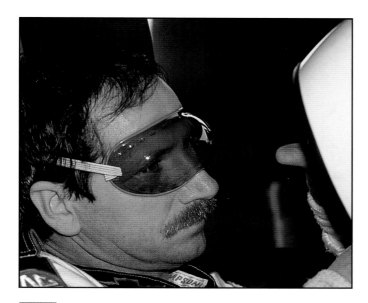

Dale Earnhardt finally got his breakthrough Daytona 500 victory in February 1998. It came in his 20th try, and it was among the most popular victories among fans and drivers in NASCAR history. The victory removed doubts about Earnhardt's "want-to" and whether he was fully recovered from a late 1997 fainting spell in the opening laps of the Southern 500.

coming back to stock cars. Combined, his two dozen or so drivers have won 43 poles and 63 races, including superspeedway events at Atlanta, Charlotte, College Station, Darlington, Daytona Beach, Dover, Ontario, Riverside, Rockingham, Talladega, and Watkins Glen.

ROD OSTERLUND: Wealthy California businessman who helped seven-time champion Dale Earnhardt get his start in Winston Cup. Osterlund fielded cars for Earnhardt one race in 1978, then the full 1979 (Rookie of the Year) and 1980 (Win-

ston Cup Championship) seasons. When he folded his team midway through the 1981 season, Earnhardt drove briefly for Jim Stacy, then finished the season with Bud Moore before moving to Richard Childress.

MARVIN PANCH: One of NASCAR earliest stars, Panch won 25 poles and 17 races in a career that spanned only 10 years between the mid-1950s and mid 1960s. Among his notable victories were the 1961 Daytona 500, the 1965 Atlanta 500 and Georgia 400 later that year, a 1965 road race at Watkins Glen, and the 1966 World 600 at Charlotte. He got eight of his career victories with the Wood brothers in the mid-1960s. His best shot at a NASCAR championship was in 1957, when he finished second to Buck Baker.

RAYMOND PARKS: A skilled and innovative mechanic, he owned and prepared the cars that won the first "Strictly Stock" NASCAR championship, forerunner of the Winston Cup. An Atlanta native, he prepared Oldsmobiles that Red Byron drove to two victories and the series championship in 1949. Earlier in his career, Parks built and tuned cars that won five Daytona Beach highway/beach races in 1947, twice each with Byron and Roy Hall, the other with Bob Flock.

BENNY PARSONS: Returned to his North Carolina roots in the late 1960s after living several years in Detroit. A part-time racer and full-time cab driver when he came South, his career resume showed 20 poles and 21 victories in 526 Winston Cup starts. Even though he won only one race and no poles along the way, he won the 1973 championship by finishing among the top-10 in almost every race. Among his 21 victories: a Daytona 500, World 600, and major victories at Atlanta, Charlotte, Darlington, Dover, Michigan, Pocono, Talladega, Ontario, Riverside, and Texas. Became a successful corporate spokesman and radio/television commentator after retiring in the early 1990s.

Jeff Gordon was an outstanding Busch Series driver before making his Winston Cup debut in the fall of 1992 near Atlanta. Although it was generally thought that Ford Motor Company had him wrapped up in a long-term deal, Chevy team owner Rick Hendrick discovered otherwise and signed Gordon for a Cup deal late in 1992. He was the 1993 Rookie of the Year and won the 1995 and 1997 Winston Cups with crew chief Ray Evernham.

David Pearson winning at the Southern 500.

Janet Guthrie after a 1977 race in Talladega on May 1, 1977. Only a handful of women have raced in Winston Cup, more of them in the early years than in the 1980s and 1990s.

New Englander Pete Hamilton made only 64 Winston Cup starts but made the most of them, winning two races at Daytona Beach and two at Talladega as a teammate to Richard Petty in 1970.

Dale Jarrett won his first Daytona 500 in 1993 with Joe Gibbs Racing, then won again in 1996 with Robert Yates Racing. Typically of modern-day Winston Cup drivers, Jarrett worked his way from weekly short-track racing through the Busch Series and into NASCAR's upper levels. His first victory came with the Wood Brothers in 1991, three years after joining the tour full-time.

Two-time NASCAR champion (1961 and 1965) Ned Jarrett become one of the sport's most successful radio/TV broadcasters after retiring from driving in the mid-1960s.

DAVID PEARSON: One of stock car racing's most successful drivers started with a bang. He won 1960 Rookie of the Year honors, then won three races his sophomore year, including the World 600 at Charlotte Motor Speedway with owner Ray Fox. He went on to win 102 more races and the 1966, 1968, and 1969 championships. His greatest success came with the Wood brothers, with whom he won 43 races driving a limited schedule between 1972 and 1979. He also won with Fox, Cotton Owens (27 races), Holman-Moody (30), Rod Osterlund (one), and Hoss Ellington (one). Even though he's second on the all-time win list (Petty won 200, Pearson 102), his 102 came in 574 starts, about half of Petty's 1,177.

ROGER PENSKE: Accepted among the most successful and powerful men in stock car racing, he owns the No. 2 Ford Taurus team featuring Rusty Wallace and operates popular, well-run, and profitable speedways in Michigan, California, and North Carolina. Better known for his involvement in Indy car racing, he's been part of NASCAR since 1972. (He left briefly in 1978 and 1979, then between 1980 and 1991). He reappeared full-time in 1991 with Wallace and team co-owner Don Miller. All told, the Penske South organization went into the 1997 season with 15 poles and 33 victories spread among Mark Donohue (one), Bobby Allison (four), and Wallace (28). Shortly before the 1998 season, he bought half of the Michael Kranefuss/Carl Haas team that features Jeremy Mayfield.

LEE PETTY: Patriarch of the first family of stock car drivers, he was among the brightest stars in NASCAR's early years. He won 18 poles and 54 races (including the first Daytona 500), and was the 1954, 1958, and 1959 series champion. His career ended in a violent crash during a qualifying race for the 1961 Daytona 500. His son, Richard, won 200 races and seven titles and his grandson, Kyle, is an eight-time Winston Cup winner. Teenage great grandsons Austin and Adam stand poised to carry the family name deep into the next century.

RICHARD PETTY: Simply put, the most successful racer in NASCAR history. But more important than that, he was stock car racing's most popular and enduring star, a humble and gracious man who never let the success of 200 victories, seven championships, and tens of millions of fans go to his head. He drove his first race in 1958 and his last in 1992, and made a record 1,177 starts in the intervening 35 years. In addition to 200 victories, 127 poles, and seven titles, he was 1959 Rookie of the Year, won eight Most Popular Driver awards, three American Driver of the Year awards, and was top-10 in points 18 times in addition to his seven titles. On superspeedways, he won 11 times at Rockingham, 10 times at Daytona Beach, seven at Dover, six at Atlanta, five each at Texas and Riverside, four each at Charlotte and Michigan, three at Darlington, and two times at Pocono and Talladega. And just for good measure, he won 145 short-track races.

TIM RICHMOND: Fans can only wonder what impact he might have had if he'd taken care of himself and raced for more than a handful of years. As it was, he won 13 races between 1982 and 1984, was winless in 1985, then won nine more in 1986 and 1987. He won his first three with Jim Stacy, another for Ray-

mond Beadle, then finished his ill-fated career with owner Rick Hendrick. But Richmond's unrestrained personal life caught up with him, and he tested HIV-positive in 1987, his last year racing.

FIREBALL ROBERTS: One of NASCAR's most popular and successful racers in the 1950s and 1960s died in 1964 several weeks after a fiery crash at the Charlotte Motor Speedway. He won 32 races and 36 poles in a career that included only 204 starts. He was at his best on superspeedways, where he had a combined nine victories at Atlanta, Darlington, and Daytona Beach. Got his nickname because he was a fastball pitcher at the University of Florida.

T. WAYNE ROBERTSON: Guided the corporate relationship between NASCAR and the R.J. Reynolds Tobacco Co. during the 1980s and 1990s. As head of RJR's wide-ranging Sports Marketing Enterprises, he was largely responsible for getting the Winston Million program and the Winston all-star race up and running. Robertson was the point man to argue that the federal government has no right to tell American adults which legally manufactured products they should be allowed to use. Died in January 1998 in a boating accident in Louisiana.

WENDELL SCOTT: The only African-American to compete regularly on the Winston Cup circuit was a skilled and competent driver who never had front-running equipment. After doing some moonshining—a dalliance not uncommon in western Virginia in the 1940s and 1950s—he took up Sportsman races on short tracks to help promoters sell tickets to minorities. His Winston Cup career lasted from the 1950s until he suffered serious injuries in a massive pileup at Talladega in 1973. Richard Pryor played him in the 1970s movie "Greased Lightning," a movie that celebrated his lone victory, at Jacksonville, Florida, in December 1963.

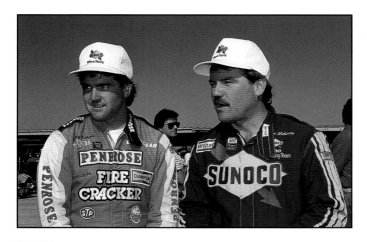

Bobby (left) and Terry Labonte are in the midst of outstanding Winston Cup careers. Bobby started the 1998 season with 5 career victories; older brother Terry has won 19 races and two Winston Cups.

One of NASCAR's earliest big stars, Fred Lorenzen drove in Grand National events from 1956 to 1973. He amassed 26 victories in 158 starts and brought home nearly $500,000 in prize money over his 17-year career. The earnings are paltry by today's standards. Jeff Gordon made more than 10 times that sum in one season.

Mark Martin has done just about everything in NASCAR racing except win the Winston Cup. Many feel it's only a matter of time.

David Pearson graduated from the rough and tumble dirt tracks of the Southeast to become a three-time NASCAR champion and one of its most successful and popular drivers. His career stats include 113 poles and 105 victories, second only to Richard Petty's 127 poles and 200 victories.

Kyle Petty is the third generation of Pettys to be successful in NASCAR Winston Cup racing.

RALPH SEAGRAVES: The man most responsible for putting Winston in Winston Cup racing was receptive when driver-turned-owner Junior Johnson came to him in 1970 asking the R.J. Reynolds Tobacco Co. to sponsor his team. Seagrave thought bigger than that, and pitched a deal to NASCAR to sponsor what was then called the Grand National circuit. They've been together since 1971, when RJR posted a modest $100,000 points fund, including $40,000 for the champion of the newly renamed Winston Cup series.

MARSHALL TEAGUE: This Daytona Beach native had some success running a limited schedule in the early 1950s. He won five races in 1950 and two the next year, then made only sporadic stock car appearances after leaving to run the USAC Champ Car circuit. He was attempting a record, in February 1959, at the brand-new Daytona International Speedway when his Indy-type car crashed at 160 miles per hour, killing him instantly.

HERB THOMAS: Despite retiring in the late 1950s after a serious crash, he's still among the top 15 in career NASCAR victories with 48, more than dozens of better-known (and better-paid) drivers. His 48 victories came between 1950 at Martinsville, Virginia, and 1956 at Merced, California, mostly in cars owned and sponsored by Carl Kiekhaefer. He was a two-time series champion, winning the 1951 and 1953 titles in his own Hudson Hornets, and was co-owner when Lee Petty won the 1954 champi-

onship. He also finished second in points three times, and was never worse than fifth every year between 1951 and 1956. He was part of Kiekhaefer's so-called "super team" that dominated the 1955 and 1956 seasons. His contribution was seven victories, far fewer than he'd won (a combined 23) with his own team the two previous seasons.

CURTIS TURNER: In the beginning, there were only a handful of recognized stars, and he was one of them. A lumberman by trade, he was sixth in the initial 1949 NASCAR standings, fifth the next year, and 10th and ninth the next two years. All told, he won 18 races between 1949 (he won the fourth race in what became the Winston Cup series) and 1959, when he quit driving to start building the Charlotte Motor Speedway. His close relationship with the Teamsters Union caused NASCAR to suspend him until 1965. He came back with a flourish, getting the final victory of his career at Rockingham in October. He was killed in a plane crash in Pennsylvania in 1970, returning to his Roanoke, Virginia, home after a business meeting in New York City.

DARRELL WALTRIP: His motto was "it ain't bragging if you can do it," and he did it more often than not. This three-time (1981, 1982, and 1985) Winston Cup champion burst into NASCAR in 1972 as either a breath of fresh air or a mouthy punk, depending on your perspective. He struggled with his own

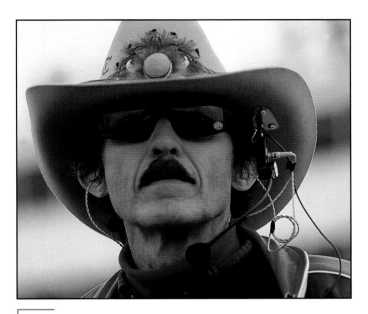

Not even the necessity of two-way radio communications with his driver keeps Richard Petty from wearing his trademark cowboy hat.

CALE YARBOROUGH: The only man to win three consecutive Winston Cups (1976, 1977 and 1978) also won 70 poles and 83 races in 559-career starts. Known for his bull-headed determination, he won with Ken Myler, the Wood brothers, Junior Johnson, M.C. Anderson, and Harry Ranier. His career began with one start in 1957 and ended after the 1988 season, when he retired to spend more time with his family and business interests. Among his most significant accomplishments: nine victories at Bristol, eight each at Daytona Beach and Michigan, seven each at Nashville, Rockingham, and Atlanta, six at Martinsville, five each at North Wilkesboro and Darlington, three each at Riverside, Charlotte, Dover, Talladega, and Richmond, two at Pocono, and one at College Station, Texas.

LEEROY YARBROUGH: One of NASCAR's best "wins-per-starts" drivers in the late 1960s and into the early 1970s. He started only 198 races and won 14 of them. His most productive years were 1964 through 1970 with owners Louie Weathersby, Jon Thorne, and Junior Johnson. Ten of his victories came on superspeedways between 1968 and 1970 in cars owned by Johnson and prepared by Herb Nab.

Tim Richmond was one of the brightest stars on the circuit until AIDS took his life on August 13, 1989. His stylish and flamboyant lifestyle did little to disguise his fiery competitive nature and undeniable place among the sport's most naturally gifted drivers.

team for several years, winning once before going to the DiGard team in the middle of 1975. He won 26 races with that team, 43 between 1981 and 1986 with owner Junior Johnson, then nine in four years with Rick Hendrick. He formed his own team for the 1991 season, and won five more races before the hard times hit in the mid-to-late 1990s. In addition to three championships, he won three NASCAR Driver of the Year and three American Driver of the Year awards. He is a two-time Most Popular Driver, won the inaugural Winston all-star race, and has 59 career poles and 84 victories, which ties him for third on the all-time list.

JOE WEATHERLY: A former national motorcycle racing champion who appeared in NASCAR in the early 1950s, won the 1962 championship with owner Bud Moore, and the 1963 title driving for several owners (including Moore and the Wood brothers). One of the sport's most popular and free-wheeling personalities of his day, he was killed early in the 1964 season in a crash at Riverside, California.

THE WOOD BROTHERS: Perhaps the most famous team in NASCAR began with brothers Leonard, Glen, and Delano, and later expanded to include sons Eddie and Len, plus some cousins and nephews. Based in Stuart, Virginia, the Wood Brothers fielded cars for Glen in 1953. He won four times in 48 starts between then and 1964, but the team was also fielding cars for other drivers during those years. Among their most famous and successful drivers: A.J. Foyt, Curtis Turner, Marvin Panch, Cale Yarborough, David Pearson, Neil Bonnet, Kyle Petty, Buddy Baker, and Dale Jarrett.

Curtis Turner and Bobby Isaac. Turner was among NASCAR's earliest stars, winning 18 races and hosting great parties (and incurring the wrath of NASCAR officials for trying to unionize drivers) throughout the 1950s and 1960s. Isaac was just the opposite—a 37-time winner and 1970 champion but something of a loner, superstitious and uncomfortable in the spotlight that Turner craved.

Three-time champion Darrell Waltrip with his 1985 Winston Cup. He also won the title in 1981 and 1982. The first of the "new wave" of young drivers to challenge the established stars of the 1950s and 1960s, the former Kentucky short-track terror burst upon the scene in the mid-1970s. Cocky, outspoken, and irreverent, he was usually as good as his word, winning with DiGard, Junior Johnson, Hendrick Motorsports, and his own team. But his last victory was at the rain-shortened Southern 500, and it seems doubtful he'll ever win again now that he's sold his team.